'Highly recommend to any adopti
guardians, teachers and any adult wi

Reading this book was like a big hug; I don't feel so alone anymore, I could relate and so much of it made sense to me. It gave me a greater understanding, knowledge and reminder of what is really going on for my children along with encouraging tools on how to move forward and make such positive change, which is possible. With life overwhelming anyway, I really love the fact this book really is a "simple" read and easy to absorb. Betsy breaks it all down perfectly into various chapters which makes it easy to jump back into at point to refer, remind and refresh myself to be the best I can be for our children.'

– Clare Davies, adoptive parent of young siblings

'Never more urgently needed, Betsy confronts this invisible but insidious issue. Offering hope and recovery, this essential read addresses compassionately and practically, the profound need in every human heart to be seen and known.'

– Nicki Rosser, Clinical Lead, TRC Bath

'Betsy's warm, wise book comes from deep knowledge of what really matters for children. Emotional neglect can be scary territory for parents and practitioners to explore and this book will support courageous conversations without shame, helping children to be seen, heard and loved. I recommend this book to everyone involved in supporting families to recover strong loving relationships.'

– Mary Glasgow, CEO of Children 1st

The
Simple Guide to
Emotional Neglect

What It Is and How to Help

Betsy de Thierry

Foreword by Dr Karen Treisman

Illustrated by Emma Reeves

Jessica Kingsley Publishers
London and Philadelphia

First published in Great Britain in 2023 by Jessica Kingsley Publishers
An imprint of John Murray Press

1

A CIP catalogue record for this title is available from the
British Library and the Library of Congress

ISBN 978 1 83997 675 9
eISBN 978 1 83997 676 6

Printed and bound in Great Britain by TJ Books Ltd

Jessica Kingsley Publishers' policy is to use papers that are natural,
renewable and recyclable products and made from wood grown in
sustainable forests. The logging and manufacturing processes are expected
to conform to the environmental regulations of the country of origin.

Jessica Kingsley Publishers
Carmelite House
50 Victoria Embankment
London EC4Y 0DZ

www.jkp.com

John Murray Press
Part of Hodder & Stoughton Limited
An Hachette UK Company

MIX
Paper from
responsible sources
FSC® C013056

CONTENTS

FOREWORD

Neglect so often gets neglected. The invisible can become further unseen. The voiceless are once again silenced.

This book does just the opposite by putting a spotlight on the crucial topic and experience of emotional neglect. By doing so, it brings to light ideas, insights and stories to help us understand its potential impact and the experiences of both children and adults who have experienced emotional neglect.

I often refer to emotional neglect as experiencing relational and emotional poverty or like being in an 'emotional and relational desert'. It is the experience of being unseen, disconnected and not held in the same way as another person, of deprivation and potentially a lack of emotional texture.

This book touches upon those children who might not have been someone's world or been fully delighted in or seen. Of course, there are many colours and shades within this subject, and in this book Betsy helpfully discusses the spectrum and the different layers of emotional neglect and how this can express itself in different ways and in different families and contexts, such as reaching out and being attention-needing to retreating and shutting-down and many other responses. Betsy draws on years of clinical experience of working with those who have experienced neglect, and she briefly presents some of the powerful studies around the possible brain-based impact of emotional neglect.

Emotional neglect can have a significant impact and far-reaching consequences and yet is something that is often hard to pin down – for example, to prove or evidence in court or to put into words – as it can be less visible and tangible. So, this book is particularly welcome as it takes the complex and multi-layered umbrella term of emotional neglect and explains it in succinct and accessible ways.

Betsy invites us to be compassionate, thoughtful and curious about these experiences. This non-blaming, non-shaming stance is supported by helpful reflective questions weaved throughout. Moreover, in busy, overstretched, under-resourced and often highly pressurized environments this book offers helpful explorations and insights written and captured in a short and simple-to-read format.

Dr Karen Treisman, clinical psychologist, trainer and author of multiple books including A Therapeutic Treasure Box for Working with Children and Adolescents with Developmental Trauma

INTRODUCTION

I have written the *Simple Guide* Series of books to simplify the important information around the impact of trauma and make it accessible to everyone. The main reason for that is to strengthen and empower the adults who are around children who have experienced trauma. When we as adults can understand the reason behind the trauma symptoms, there can be hope for children to recover, and both adults and children can live with less stress, and be more empowered for a positive future.

My aim for this book is that it prevents some children having to endure emotionally distressing experiences, and equally validates those children and adults who have had to endure them. The books are also written to help people from all walks of life to grasp how trauma recovery can be found so that we can build positive, affirming and supportive communities for all.

This book is about emotional neglect and emotional unmet needs across the continuum of distress. This is a subject that can be difficult to speak about or explore because it is so invisible, and any discussion or reflection can depend on being able to know and compare with that which is perceived as 'normal'. It is written for a wide-ranging group of people, including adoptive parents who know that their child probably had a history of emotional neglect; adults who recognize that their childhood was possibly one that was marked by that experience too and want to explore the impact and recovery route; and parents of children who experienced painful interruptions to the plans of life, where they found that they were unable to be as emotionally available and as nurturing as they had hoped, maybe due to ill health or a significant crisis of some kind. I am also hoping that those of us who have parented with our absolute best effort, but look and wonder what went a little wrong, could be humble enough to explore the possibility that the invisible but powerful lack of *enough* emotional connection and co-regulating can lead to their child struggling with some trauma symptoms – and the book is very much *not* wanting to point any fingers or shame or blame, but bring hope that recovery is possible.

The term 'parents' will be mostly used throughout for simplicity, because otherwise the words can be rather lumpy when we use the many different possibilities of primary caregivers such as carers, guardians and other adults. Usually, I like to use adults as the term within my books to describe a key role for children, but in this book I think it's important to recognize the role of the parent or the parent-type role.

There are so many life experiences that as adults we don't seem to be able to control, no matter how much we want to, and some of these can lead to a child not being able to access enough of the relational support they need. As we explore that in this book, I hope that you will be able to do so with an open mind and heart, and one that can be brave enough to explore the possibilities of emotional trauma occurring, so that recovery can be experienced for all.

When we can understand our humanity and what our needs were and are without shame, recovery can begin.

It is complex being a human and the more we understand about how we are wired and what our needs are, the more we are able to accept what we need and recover from the pain of trauma. Psychoeducation is life changing because it empowers us where we have often been powerless and helps us move forward with tools for recovery.

Well done for exploring this issue and not pretending it's not there!

Betsy x

Chapter One

AN INTRODUCTION TO EMOTIONAL NEGLECT

How our brains are built

A baby's brain develops rapidly, starting from when they are inside the womb and then continuing to grow throughout childhood. This early brain growth becomes the foundation of health and wellbeing for the child and impacts every area of their life as they mature into adulthood. The reciprocal interactions that take place between the baby and their parent facilitate the early, speedy development of the brain, especially in the first three years. It's the positive, repetitive, rewarding relationships that create healthy neural connections that lead to healthy mental wellbeing. When the baby has 'enough' of the reciprocal, positive, rewarding experiences of emotional connection with the adults who care for them, they develop a solid foundation of brain architecture that can support the developing child's growth in learning, relationships and emotions. When a baby or child doesn't have 'enough' of these positive, repetitive experiences, and they instead experience prolonged unresponsiveness from their parent, it can activate their stress responses, because they feel frightened and are powerless to get the help and support they need. This stress can have significant impact on their brain's development, their nervous system and emotional and physical health. We know that emotional neglect, especially in the first three to five years, can have significant impact on the child's life as it is known as a 'sensitive period' of brain development and fast growth (Schore 2002). This is a big motivation for why early responses to emotional neglect can be so important and life changing. Researchers do recognize that brain development continues throughout childhood and there is a high level of 'plasticity' until early adulthood, when it starts to decrease.

But recovery is possible, and the younger the recovery journey can start, the easier it can be to see neurobiological changes occur due to new positive, relational, repetitive experiences that rewire some parts of the brain that need the attention.

The continuum of emotional neglect

Emotional neglect and unmet emotional needs seem to be experiences that people can't always easily understand, comprehend or empathize with, even though we know that the primary experience for the baby and child of not having an emotionally connected adult is being terrified, powerless and overwhelmed.

There is a whole continuum of emotional neglect. It starts on one end with the distress and stress that a child experiences when they have unmet emotional needs. On the other end of the continuum, where the child is caused deep distress by the unmet emotional needs and the consequences of that distress are then seen in behaviours, emotions and trauma symptoms, emotional neglect can be a criminal offence. Child emotional neglect at the most severe end of the continuum is also defined as child cruelty and therefore child abuse, due to the level of deprivation. It is vital that we don't refuse to notice what we see to 'avoid judgement' when we suspect that a child is in a situation such as this, but instead it is vital to immediately involve child protection services (police and social workers) who need to help the child urgently. Often in situations where neglect is the issue, adults around them can unintentionally collude with the neglect and can become apathetic to the obvious needs of the child (Wolock & Horowitz 1984). We recognize that whilst 'removal' from those settings is not in any way the whole answer, it can be an important factor for the child's safety and can reduce the further impact of developmental trauma. Further along the emotional neglect continuum would be the desperate lack of emotional connection which can feel like a matter of life and death to a child, although they would rarely be able to put that into words. At the other end of the continuum the child has unmet emotional needs that lead to coping mechanisms that can be interruptive to their healthy development.

Emotional neglect could be explained as the ongoing lack of emotional responsiveness to the child, where the parent doesn't notice what the child may be feeling, doesn't try to help them explore what may be going on and doesn't validate their experiences enough. The child feels that their feelings are consistently ignored, unvalidated and disregarded by their parent.

The official definitions of emotional neglect used in law can be found in the Appendix.

Emotional trauma

Emotional neglect leads to emotional trauma, which is a word used interchangeably with psychological trauma, to differentiate it from physical traumatic injury that requires surgeons, doctors and medics to facilitate healing:

> Trauma is defined as any experience or repeated experience where the child feels terrified, powerless and overwhelmed and that challenges their capacity to cope. It leaves an imprint on the person's nervous system, emotions, body, behaviours, learning and relationships. What is traumatic for one individual may not be traumatic for another, but the degree of impact of the trauma is usually connected to the child's ability to find comfort and reassurance from a safe and known adult in the aftermath of the experience. (de Thierry 2020, p.21)

Emotional trauma is the experience that causes terror, powerlessness and overwhelm and leads to behaviours and coping mechanisms which help the person survive. When a child feels terrified and powerless, they are dependent on adults helping them, and emotional neglect is an experience where the adult hasn't been able to offer that support and care, and so the child is left feeling isolated, overwhelmed and terrified. There seems to be less of a universal understanding of the impact of the often-invisible traumatic experiences of emotional neglect and unmet emotional needs, and so they are often not acknowledged or validated. Often those who have lived through these experiences can struggle to use words to effectively describe how devastating their experience has been. Many children growing up may not even be aware of anything being wrong with their lives, because it has been their normal. Sometimes the person growing up is aware of their coping mechanisms or overwhelming feelings of shame or self-rejection or other difficult feelings, but may find it hard to express what trauma they have survived.

We know that as humans we seem to find that bruises elicit less empathy than wounds with blood, even if the bruise is life-threatening, and emotional trauma can often feel like that.

'I lied and told the teacher my friend's mum had died of cancer, because I couldn't answer her question about why I was always sighing in class and struggling to concentrate. I didn't know what or if anything was wrong with me. I guess I just knew I was sad and felt overwhelmed.'

Sophie, aged 16, who grew up with emotional neglect

The experience of emotional neglect

As has been explained, childhood emotional neglect is on a continuum that starts with a situation where the child's emotional needs were not quite met enough, and then stretches onto the other end to child cruelty, such as the shocking institutional neglect that we read about in research from orphanages in Romania (Marshall, Fox & the BEIP Core Group 2004) or in family homes which have similar settings.

It is a prolonged and repetitive experience in childhood where the child doesn't have their emotional needs met fully, doesn't understand their emotions and is left feeling confused or disconnected and not really seen or heard. It can be hard to know what is 'good enough' and what is enough time spent being emotionally present with children and it would be natural for parents to feel defensive, as if we are about to be judged and blamed for anything that our children experienced. It's important to re-emphasize that we recognize most of us are trying to do our best in life and usually any mistakes are due to our own trauma and unprocessed childhood and it's usually not too late to facilitate some positive change in most relationships.

Children rarely have words to describe the experience of childhood neglect and that leads to further lack of care, validation, empathy, additional support or kindness from adults, because people don't 'see' where they are suffering.

I have always argued that one of worst elements of the trauma of emotional neglect can be due to adults around the child not being able to recognize what's going on and therefore assuming that the trauma symptoms on display in the child's behaviour are due to 'naughtiness' or 'bad choices'. This leaves the child further distressed, often isolated and feeling abandoned and this can cause the trauma symptoms and pain and distress to increase. Although society can often present maltreatment and abuse as the biggest source of turmoil for a child, we actually know from psychological research that:

> For a baby, the most painful experience of all seems to be not being able to get mothers attention. Babies make the most protest when their mother's attention is switched off, as if this is even more unbearable than maltreatment. (Gerhardt 2004, p.124)

Research suggests that emotional neglect, where the child cannot get the emotional connection that they need, could be more harmful than other childhood experiences such as physical abuse (Pollak *et al*. 2000).

We aren't shaming and blaming – but we are acknowledging the impact

There are so many possible settings and family cultures that could breed emotional unmet needs and many adults would be horrified to think that this book could suggest that they may have neglected their child. Very few adults would choose to hurt their child and so it's usually due to generational trauma that unmet emotional needs occur. For example, the adult parent also experienced childhood emotional pain and hadn't processed their own trauma and so continued to parent in a way that felt similar and familiar. Adults don't generally choose to be emotionally unavailable and pre-occupied with their own survival; adults don't choose to be physically bed-bound or substance-abusing and many parents are doing the best with the experiences they have had. We recognize that for the majority of adults, they will parent how they were parented unless they have made a specific decision to stop the generational norms and reassess the parenting traditions and cultures. This would often mean that they were able to access the support they needed to unpack their own traumatic childhood experiences of what did or didn't happen to them, but we all know that finding that support can be difficult or costly. So, the pages of this book need to be read with gentle kindness and not judgement, as we recognize some of the settings that have caused pain for many, so that we can begin to be able to move forward rather than be stuck in the past. It's really important that we don't simplify this too much, and that we recognize that every family and parent is in a unique position. Many parents have tried their best within some of these settings to emotionally nurture and emotionally connect to their child and so we must never use such a list as a weapon to judge and criticize those who are trying their best in the situations they find themselves. Let's use the information to recognize how important it is to offer support to those who need it, for their own sake and also for their children. Gabor Maté, who speaks about these vital early days, months and years in a baby's development, states that they 'establish either a sturdy or fragile foundation for all the health, learning and behaviour that follows' (Maté 2021).

What is 'good enough'?

In 1971, the great British psychoanalyst Donald Winnicott created the term 'good enough parenting' to conceptualize the need for a child to experience consistent availability and predictability from their caring adult but that 'it is normal for fluctuations in the provision of attention and awareness' (de Thierry 2015, p.57). Winnicott states that: 'perfection belongs to machines, and the imperfections that are characteristic of human adaptation to need are an essential quality in the environment that facilitates' (2005, p.187) and that is not the expectation for a parent.

Edward Tronick's research in the 1970s and 80s was also incredibly helpful as he gives us a sense of what is 'enough'. His studies in the parent and child relationship of emotional attention draws the conclusion that the parents who were really trying to meet the needs of their babies were in tune and responded with something that seemed to soothe the child around 20 to 30 per cent of the time, but there was a lot of 'working out' what on earth the baby needed and the baby was often crying or was frustrated at these attempts, which were therefore not met with relief but frustration. The research points to the power of resolution after the distressing lack of ability to soothe, and how that repair and resolve can strengthen the child's sense of feeling known, nurtured and safe. So, the aim is not for perfection in parenting, emotional connection and soothing, but to keep trying even when it seems to not go well, even if it seems worse momentarily, because the attempts are understood as a desire to support and help.

A job description for an emotionally connecting parent could be that they:

> afford emotional access to the child and responds appropriately and promptly to his or her positive or negative states. She allows for the interactive generation of high levels of positive affect in co-shared play states, and low levels of negative affect in the interactive repair of social stress, i.e. attachment ruptures. (Schore 2001, p.12)

Some people talk about children being resilient, but I would argue that their measure of resilience matches the degree of emotional connection, safety and strength of the relationship they have with their parent. They become resilient *because* they feel safe with their attachment figure and so can take risks and explore the world, knowing they can come back to their safety.

What kind of specific experiences could be emotionally neglectful?

- Parents who are not emotionally available to build a relationship with the child.

- Self-absorbed parents who show little interest in the child.

- Parents who are unable to be consistently available due to mental health challenges.

- Parents who are unable to be predictable and available due to drugs/alcohol.

- Emotionally immature parents.

- Parents who use screens to babysit their child for hours and hours.

- Traditional authoritarian parents with verbally aggressive 'discipline'.

- Parents who are too busy (with siblings/work/their interests).

- Parents who struggle with being suicidal for some time.

- Parents who arrange constant childcare but are not available enough themselves.

- When there are other siblings that have additional needs and so there is limited time available.

- When there has been birth trauma.

- When there has been a separation from parents due to war/disaster/prison.

- Parents who are busy with work/practical tasks/looking after another adult.

- Parents who never had emotional connection so didn't know how to give it.

- Parents who believe that the child should learn to be independent from early on.

- Parents in the midst of their own trauma of domestic abuse, poverty, harassment, etc.

- The child parenting the parents or feeling responsible for them.

- A child being neither seen nor heard.

- A home where emotions are not allowed, encouraged or validated.

- A parent who never wanted their child and either

tells them that or behaves in ways that make the child believe they are unwanted.

- A parent who can't regulate their own emotions.

- A child that never feels like they belong and can't seem to work out the 'rules' to fit in.

What we know is that whatever we experience and interpret as love as children, is what we believe love is. So therefore, if a child was ignored or told to be silent and perfect, or if the child was teased and mocked, or if they were told that they were responsible for everyone, then that is how they may interpret love and that can cause some long-term challenges in relationships because:

> sometimes, of course, it is not the mother's absence that is the problem for the child, but the quality of her presence. Even if children are at home with their biological parents, they may still be poorly regulated. For example, children of alcoholic parents have high levels of cortisol, probably as a result of having parents who may be physically present, but mentally unavailable to provide consistent regulation (Jackson *et al.* 1999). (Gerhardt 2004, p.75)

The child being seen and heard

Emotional neglect and unmet emotional needs are primarily about the child not feeling seen and heard, and the child's feelings not being noticed or validated regularly enough. This causes the child to learn to hide them and pull away from the adults to keep some kind of emotional distance, or pretend they are fine or happy. Often, they do this because the adult hasn't learnt to listen to their own feelings or express them in a healthy way and so their natural reaction towards negative emotions is to push them down or ignore them and this becomes the culture of the home.

Some parents can often have no idea they are neglecting their children's emotions because it feels normal to them to ignore emotions. They may be very committed and intentional parents but don't have a grasp on the importance of emotional literacy to lead to emotional and mental wellbeing. The families often look 'good enough' outwardly and they may all seem happy and chatty with plenty of toys and after school opportunities in abundance. They may however, struggle to be able to talk openly about how they feel, what's really going on at school and what worries them, so that it doesn't become normal to express a negative emotion and be soothed and comforted and feel relief in the presence of an adult who cares.

What do children need from their parents?

What we know with confidence is that parents and carers are very much needed to be emotionally present to co-regulate the child from birth until they can regulate their own emotions. The main four roles of parenting seem to be attunement, validation, containment and soothing. My six Cs are in sequential order and are care, connect, co-regulate, calm, comfort and then consider. Dan Siegel uses his four Ss of parenting; making sure the child is seen, safe, soothed and secure (Siegel & Payne Bryson 2020).

When the adult is able to be repetitively emotionally available for the child, the consequence is that the child doesn't need to use subconscious or conscious coping mechanisms to cope with their daily new experiences and emotions, but are able instead to relax back into the safety and trust of their parent. When there has been an interruption to the positive emotional connection in the relationship, this can be repaired in the same way that a lot of other relational restoration occurs – through repetitive positive relational experiences, alongside the ability to create space to reflect on things that haven't gone so well.

> From birth the parent responds to the then explicit needs of the child. Whilst there is a natural recognition of the vulnerability of the baby that causes most people older than the baby to respond with a strong protective reaction, attachment is a specific response that: provides safety and security; regulates emotions by comforting, creating joy, and helping to facilitate calm; offers a secure base from which to explore 'the world'. (de Thierry 2019, p.15)

The need to provide emotional availability for children and teens

We know that a baby develops a healthy expectation of other people when they spend the first five years especially being immersed in faces smiling at them in delight, eyes that gleam and adore. When this is a regular experience, the baby basks in that sense of being loved, feeling wanted and known, and develops an expectation that other people will feel the same way in their presence. When a child hasn't had 'enough' of this foundational and moulding experience that enables healthy brain development, they can grow up confused about who they are, where they fit in and how to be seen by others; often preferring to shrink back to avoid eye contact or be in control of the crowd, or oscillating between both.

In a training day that I facilitate, I regularly ask adults what the children they work with have said about why they haven't told their parents when something bad has happened to them, what worries them or how they are feeling and they always say the same kind of things. I think it's a sad list and one we can all use to intentionally make sure we can be emotionally available to children:

- Their parents aren't around.

- Their parents have other worries.

- Their parents are caught up in their own world.

- Their parents are too busy.

- The child knows the additional stress parents are under.

- They feel that their worries seem trivial in comparison to their parents' worries.

- Their parents seem overwhelmed and emotionally unavailable.

- They would worry about the impact of talking to their parents, and so they don't want to add to their stress.

- Their parents are not available physically or emotionally.

'I didn't know I was emotionally neglected; I just knew my mum was ill (sectioned as mentally unwell) and we were always just thinking about how to not cause additional stress for her. I grew up unaware of having any needs and trying to be as good as possible so I didn't cause any problems. I can now see looking back that I was terrified all the time that it would be my fault if she died, because I was too demanding or noisy – so I was just good and quiet. No one in my home really knew me.'

James, an adult survivor of emotional neglect

Emotional neglect occurs across all socio-economic family backgrounds

Having unmet emotional needs is a traumatic experience that occurs across the socio-economic spectrum of families. The child grows up wondering 'what is wrong with them' as they face challenges that seem to make no sense. A child with parents who are struggling to be emotionally present when exhausted because of working long hours to meet the needs of the family; or a child sent to boarding school, feeling lonely, confused and abandoned; a child left alone with the TV without anyone noticing their needs, or surrounded by people but not really 'known' – the exact situations can differ, but the lack of positive, repetitive, warm, reciprocal relational connection is the theme, and the feeling of disconnection and shock is familiar, whilst the coping mechanisms can be worlds apart. There is a wide range of coping mechanisms, from dominating and controlling others to hiding, withdrawing and people-pleasing, and many others.

Generational emotional trauma zig zag

When a child was ignored and didn't feel emotionally connected, as adults they often raise their children in the same way unless they have realized the negative impact and then they may do the opposite and can be over-protective or smothering of their own child in order to avoid what they hated. When a child is over-protected, controlled or 'managed' too much, as an adult, if they realize that, they may then raise their children with too few boundaries or too little time spent with each other. I call this the generational zig zag. It is a common pattern when we recognize that what we experienced wasn't quite good enough, so we try and do better, but we then can over-balance the other way unless we have others around us who we can reflect with.

Being curious about our expectations and norms is the first starting point of change and understanding the impact of experiences on our emotions, behaviour, relationships and body is the next stage towards positive change and recovery.

Reflection points

- What would you describe as essential elements of 'good enough' emotional connection?

- Have you ever heard anyone try and explain a difficult childhood without many words? Were you able to validate that?

- Have you known a child who was possibly emotionally neglected? How did they behave?

Chapter Two

THE GENERAL IMPACT OF EMOTIONAL NEGLECT

The impact of emotional neglect is primarily on the child's long-term subconscious understanding of relationships, on their emotions, on their learning, on their sense of self and on their brain and body. It's an experience that can be deeply stressful and can cause neurobiological changes to the child due to their dependence on adults for everything. Let's explore some possible consequences of experiencing emotional neglect, and what the impact may look like for the child whose developing years were marked by 'not enough' emotional connection, repetition, consistency, availability and gentle attuned nurture.

What we do need to hold in mind as we explore the impact is that there is hope for change, despite the child's experience. It's easier to heal and restore before adulthood, but recovery is entirely possible in adulthood with some hard work and the right support, and the recovery journey has similar elements to it.

The impact of not having a secure attachment

We recognize that attachment theory (Bowlby 1973) helps us to understand that in these early years, the parent's role is to intentionally build a long-term, healthy, emotional connection, which is called an attachment relationship. Attachment theory helps us to understand that our experience of an adult(s) caring for us, in the first five years especially, forms a subconscious internal template for all future relationships. If the attachment relationships were terrifying, this may cause a disorganized attachment internal template where the child experiences the instinctive drive for emotional connection with the parent, whilst simultaneously feeling fearful or nervous to be too close to them. If the attachment experience was not 'enough' to fulfil the child's needs for emotional closeness and to feel seen and heard, then that lack of soothing, comfort and repetitive, positive and warm interactions can lead to an anxious, ambivalent, avoidant or insecure attachment internal template. These negative attachment templates can cause deep distress. The more 'avoidant' style of attaching is a common consequence of emotional neglect because the child hasn't had enough positive experiences and yet has an increasing sense of desperate need within them. In Tronick and colleagues' (1975) still face experiment, the child who had an avoidant attachment doesn't seem to be bothered by the parent coming or leaving, but:

> …their physiology gives them away. When they are separated, their heart-rates and cortisol levels shoot up. We do not see their distress, and they to do not seem to know that they are distressed. They lack (or have lost) the ability to read their own emotional-bodily signals. (Music 2022)

The other important consequence of attachment relationships that are not consistent and nurturing enough is that the child doesn't get enough practice of co-regulation. This means they can grow up lacking some of the opportunities for the appropriate development of the skills that help build the positive relationships that are needed for healthy lives. They seem to show a lack of empathy or ability to understand others' emotions and therefore can often become lonely, withdrawn and isolated. Gerhardt describes the impact of the lack of secure attachment relationships in the early years, by explaining that, 'instead of actively solving problems with other people, talking things through, confident that some resolution can be found, they tend either to withdraw from people or attack them aggressively' (Gerhardt 2004, p.130).

Babies and children who have not had enough co-regulation can grow up afraid of being seen as vulnerable, because that can feel too terrifying and can cause them to feel that there is probable rejection. The fear of being vulnerable and being known by another person can lead to many different coping mechanisms; these include the desperate need for people's time and attention or hiding, withdrawing and being compliant or expressing intense emotions that they hope will lead to emotional connection with someone.

The impact in adulthood

Often adults wonder why they are left with crippling insecurity, a sense of void internally, anxiety or depression that seems to come from nowhere. They can also be confused at a pattern of repeated relationship struggles. They often describe their childhoods as 'not that bad compared to others' and often cannot recall trauma in the way that they hear others describe it. Often, they even say 'Well, I wasn't abused was I?'. What we know, however, is that when a child is not able to be emotionally supported by their parents, it can often leave them feeling very deeply alone or confused. Sometimes they learn that pleasing an adult can bring connection, and so the cycle of people-pleasing begins and becomes normalized throughout adulthood. Sometimes focusing on avoiding adults' anger and negative emotion can be learnt in early childhood, and therefore that becomes the norm in adulthood, but leaves the person feeling alone, isolated and confused about strong emotions. Sometimes the drive to be known and to be emotionally connected can lead to being exploited and manipulated by others who have learnt to recognize the signs of such an emotional void in others.

The impact of lack of soothing

One of the primary roles of the parent is to nurture and soothe and communicate with the child in a way that enables them to feel emotionally safe. The child needs to experience repetitive co-regulation – where the child expresses something and the adult responds to it, validates it and helps them resolve it. Sometimes this is called the 'serve and return' experience of relationships. Repetitive co-regulation leads to self-regulation. Parents who are not able to co-regulate their children can end up leaving the child in a distressed state for too long. Sometimes this is due to the adult's sense of overwhelm due to the consistent needs of the non-verbal baby who is trying to communicate with loud cries or the toddler's loud and demonstrative expression of emotion. The sound of the baby crying or a toddler screaming with frustration does cause distress to the caregiver and causes them to want to quickly attend to them; but when they are unable to do so, it can cause both the child and parent significant distress by the lack of comfort and resolve. The more times that the child isn't able to quickly receive the comfort they need so urgently, the more they are likely to be more sensitive to the slightest delay or feeling of being ignored and therefore react with even more urgency, which can mean louder screams and more demonstrative attention-grabbing behaviour or eventually they may shut down and give up. It's normal for the parent to not be able to always immediately comfort the baby when it cries, but when a child is left crying for long periods of time without comfort, there can be considerable damage.

waa waa

The distress of relationships that have insecure foundations

As the neglected baby or child gets older, they have usually developed a few instinctive, automatic possible reactions to feeling distress; to help them stay alive in what feels like a life and death situation. The baby or child either has to move into some kind of shutting down, so that the distress no longer causes pain and turmoil but is instead separated from the feeling of distress, which is called dissociation; or they learn that they need to work hard to receive the attention they need for survival, and become increasingly demonstrative, frustrated and angry, demanding their needs are met. There are lots of possible behaviours which are either internalized or externalized that can be due to unmet needs causing distress that feels overwhelming. This can then cause the adults in the midst of a child's frequent emotional outburst to also feel overwhelmed, and they can either feel powerless and want to give up and walk away or they can 'snap' and be angry. Sadly, the child is then left feeling further abandoned and frightened, which can escalate their responses. It can be that both parent and baby feel like they are trapped in a cycle of distress with little emotional energy to work out a solution. If the parent is able to keep trying to comfort the distressed baby and toddler, they can then become sensitive to any loud noises or emotional outbursts, and excitement and happy sounds can cause the same feeling of panic. The parents may find exuberance and playful behaviour can feel uncontrollable, and so rather than share with the child's delight, they can shame, blame, mock or tell off the children, causing further confusion, abandonment and sadness.

The impact of the lack of 'enough' emotional attunement

When an adult isn't able to tune into or 'step into the shoes' of the child to be curious about what they may be needing, the child can feel misunderstood and not 'known'. They rarely develop words to ask for that experience of being known and so instead display behaviour that shows they are distressed, or clingy, or rejecting, but if they are asked, will not know why or how their distress can be 'solved'. Children are dependent on the parent tuning into them and helping them explore their feelings and then model emotional language around what they may be feeling and what they can do to resolve the discomfort of the feelings. When a child has this experience regularly, with both positive and negative feelings, they begin to be able to use emotional language themselves and understand themselves and their reactions more. When this is a repetitive experience in their first five years, then they are able to grow up with more confidence and understanding of who they are, what they feel and how they can move from a state of distress to a place of calm. This is a secure foundation from which to build relationships with others and continue to learn about themselves and their place in the world.

The good news is that when a child hasn't had enough of these experiences for whatever reason, there is still hope for the child to have enough experiences in their childhood or early adulthood for change to be possible, whilst the brain is still developing and is therefore very malleable. An adult can facilitate the growth and healing of a child's brain by providing that consistent, kind, attuned, nurturing relationship where the child can feel emotionally safe enough to explore how they are feeling. The older they get, the more repetitions they need and the harder it can be to find ways to emotionally connect – but it is still possible. A secondary attachment figure in a school or club is incredibly helpful to support the primary attachment relationship. We know that 'they can learn new attachment behaviours as they experience positive, repetitive, affirming, nurturing relationships with adults. The co-regulation and emotional attunement that we explored earlier is the pathway to a child developing a healthy brain, subconscious and future' (de Thierry 2019, p.60).

The impact of emotionally shut down parents

Some parents can be so stuck in their own world where emotions seem like enemies or strangers that they aren't able to use empathy to attune to their child and reflect on how they may be feeling and offer appropriate comfort. This can lead to the child feeling alone and scared, wondering what they are feeling and what's wrong with them. They could then become further shut down or desperate to find coping mechanisms to help them cope with their distress.

When the parent is stuck emotionally in anxiety, depression or a current traumatic experience, they can struggle to play with their child, or respond to 'banter' or silliness and fun in the house, and may instead strive for an emotionally calm environment where they feel more in control and neither anger nor hilarity is expressed. The child may grow up wanting to please their parents in order to gain some emotional connection and so they suppress their feelings, but that can also lead them to try and please other adults to reach emotional connection too. We know that generally people-pleasers started off as parent-pleasers.

'I knew I was sad and couldn't talk but the only thing I could think of saying was that a neighbour had cancer and so I was sad. The teacher was then kind to me and although I felt like I had lied, at least it seemed like I had a reason for my deep sadness that I couldn't seem to speak about.'

Luke, aged 13, who was emotionally neglected

The impact of the child worrying about their parent

When a child grows up with a parent who depends on them and whom they worry about, the impact can also be damaging in the long term. The child can end up having to adapt their behaviour, hide their emotions and limit their own interests to make sure that the adult has their needs met. Sometimes of course, this can serve to help the child develop extraordinary patience and kindness, but if they feel the weight of responsibility for the wellbeing of their parent, it can be damaging. A parent who struggles to regulate their own feelings of distress could find it difficult to tolerate the child's distress and their need for soothing. The child can pick up on this lack of resource available and want to protect their adult from further distress and thus they swop into the caring role and begin to parent their parent whilst pushing down any of their own needs and emotions.

Possible consequences of not enough emotional connection from parents

The child can grow up:

- not wanting to take up space

- with behaviour that seems younger than the biological age
- with feelings of isolation and emotional loneliness
- feeling a sense of abandonment and trying to make sense of the world alone
- dissociating (ranging severity from depersonalization, derealization to dissociative identity disorder (DID))
- with depression and anxiety and other mental health challenges
- having social difficulties with friendships and expectations
- providing self-sacrificial care for everyone else and self-neglecting
- looking at other families to see emotional connection to learn what it is
- trying to be invisible
- looking for acceptance that they weren't given
- looking for safety, felt in the body that they didn't experience at a core level
- with a lack of patience with themselves as adults were always impatient with them
- with a lack of learning and education due to struggling to focus due to needing to survive
- with a need for respect from others as they never felt respected

- showing passive, withdrawn and aggressive behaviour patterns with their parents

- suffering from child development delay, failure to thrive

- exhibiting disruptive, impulsive behaviour, including aggression

- with low self-esteem and self-compassion

- with deep feelings of shame

- in severe cases, developing coping mechanisms such as rocking and self-soothing.

What we do know is that when a child feels deeply known, loved, seen and heard by their parent, then they begin to be able to explore who they are. It's from that 'safe base' that they are able to explore, learn, grow and develop in every aspect of life. This can take continual repetitive, consistent, attuned, nurturing care which can be exhausting – but it does facilitate life-changing recovery. The nurture they experience is the foundation to throw themselves into learning, relationships and growth. Without this foundation of consistent emotionally available nurture, children either freeze, shut down and observe life from a distance, or are constantly on alert for signs of threat and ready to fight and defend their vulnerable self that feels so unprotected. Emotional neglect across the continuum can cause the child to feel terrified, powerless and overwhelmed, navigating themselves in a big wide world where they feel alone.

My formal description of the neurobiological impact of emotional neglect

Research recognizes that there is a link between emotional neglect and adverse cognitive and socioemotional outcomes. Emotional neglect causes neurobiological changes that hinder the brain and body's natural development, and impact behaviour, cognition, emotional regulation, relationships and learning. The younger that the child experiences emotional neglect, the more likely they are to experience neurobiological damage to the developing brain (Mueller *et al.* 2010; Salokangas 2021; Shonkoff *et al.* 2012).

The amygdala (see the Glossary for more information on parts of the brain) is situated in the limbic region of the brain. Its main function is in emotional responses, including feelings of happiness and fear and anger. It becomes enlarged when a child experiences neglect, due to hypervigilance and the continual threat of danger, which is due to lack of consistent adult protection. This leads to a heightened fear response, being easily startled, struggling to settle to learn due to adrenaline and agitation (Aust *et al.* 2014; Pechtel *et al.* 2014; Tottenham *et al.* 2010, 2011).

The prefrontal cortex is usually underdeveloped and shows as smaller in MRI scans of neglected adults and teenagers, and this can hinder their cognition, ability to think and reflect and other executive functions, such as planning, monitoring, working memory, problem-solving and self-regulation (Frodl *et al.* 2010; Lupien *et al.* 2011).

The corpus callosum can be underdeveloped due to emotional neglect. The primary function of the corpus callosum is to integrate and transfer information from both cerebral hemispheres to process sensory, motor, and high-level cognitive signals. This can lead to a lack of ability to use words to ask for help, describe feelings and emotionally connect with others, and causes feelings of overwhelm which can lead to impulsive behaviours, depression and other trauma symptoms (Mehta *et al.* 2009; Teicher *et al.* 2004).

The hippocampus also has reduced volume and this impacts learning and memory. The stress of emotional neglect can also reduce the hippocampus' ability to facilitate the lowering of cortisol levels (McCrory, De Brito & Viding 2011; Shonkoff *et al.* 2012).

Reflection points

- How can we spot these children and help them reduce their coping mechanisms despite their experiences?

- How can we help reduce the probable trauma symptoms that otherwise will be carried with them through their life?

- What neurobiological changes have you found to be most obvious in children or adults you know who have a history of emotional neglect or emotional unmet needs?

Chapter Three

THE IMPACT OF EMOTIONAL NEGLECT ON RELATIONSHIPS

Children need to feel secure and safe in the knowledge that they have an adult who looks after them and knows what they need. They need to be able to explore their world with the confident expectation that an adult will keep them safe and will be eager to be a guide and a safe place through all the experiences and emotions that will arise. The child needs to feel that they are wanted, loved, valued and delighted in. Relationships have the power to harm and to heal.

When a child has grown up with the feeling that they are not fully known, seen and heard, they can end up having a dysfunctional understanding of relationships in their subconscious which can lead to different ways of coping and surviving the resulting deep distress that cannot often be expressed verbally. It's hard for humans to express the sadness of what they may have never had, when they are not sure what that should have been! For some children there is just a sense of feeling a lack of ease in relationships due to lack of early, foundational experience, this can lead to confusion. Music (2022) describes an emotionally neglected child who 'barely noticed social cues and easily went under people's radars' (pp.64–65).

Let's explore some of the different consequences and

possible coping mechanisms that can operate within relationships where emotional neglect or unmet emotional needs have been a theme, especially in the early years.

Being invisible

When the child has not had repetitive, consistent emotional connection, they can end up being unsure of how to emotionally connect with others and can have little understanding of the nuances of relational interaction. This can sometimes cause them to feel clumsy and awkward as they go between saying what they think, and then withdrawing, needing to feel invisible and silent for fear of further feelings of rejection. They may soon give up with saying what they think. They can feel as if they are invisible because children who are more confident, who have had 'enough' repetitive relational interaction can fully throw themselves into playing and laughing, confident to navigate themselves through the ups and downs of connection whilst often not seeming to understand why others can't seem to work out the unwritten rules and boundaries of 'normal relationship behaviour'. The longer the child who has been emotionally neglected has to wait for an adult to offer experiences of positive, repetitive relational interactions where they can learn these skills, the more they may learn coping mechanisms to help them cope with the discomfort that they feel. This period, where the emotional discomfort is pushed down and where the world can seem to move around them with speed, can then lead them to be further pushed into isolation and feeling forgotten about as they silently look on with envy and sadness at the innocent playing of their classmates. The feeling of being invisible or an observer in the cinema showing of their own life can cause them to feel distress or numb as they look on with slight detached confusion.

> These children need to have some gentle narrating of their life with a focus on validating their feelings, including negative and scary ones so they feel fully seen and accepted.

Not being a person, not taking up space

When the needs of the adult take more airspace in the family home than the child's, they can very quickly learn that it's best to 'bottle up' their feelings and worries in order to support their adult. The child can grow up knowing instinctively that no one noticed when they needed emotional support and no one seemed to be available to help them explore what their needs are. This can mean that the child learnt to keep their emotions hidden, not ask for help and not take up space or be seen as a burden or inconvenience to the greater needs of the adults that need their support. When there is an opportunity to be centre stage, to be seen and heard, they may feel insecure, threatened or anxious about people looking at them and what the expectation could be, because the experience can feel so unfamiliar and new. Children who grow up with adults who are not able to be emotionally connected with them can often feel like they are not a person, because they can feel numb and conflicted and hide or freeze to survive. Often this can lead to them not being noticed, as they stay quietly looking on at others. When a child has had repetitive experiences of telling their stories with adults listening intently, or when they can express heartfelt emotions with the full attention and soothing of an adult, they are less nervous about 'taking up space' in other relationships and can confidently explore their feelings with others who can offer validation and soothing.

> These children need help to be seen in a way where shame is intentionally decreased and a positive reception is guaranteed. They need to know that their needs can take up space and no one falls apart when they need that space.

Being responsible for too much

A child who learns that their needs should be hidden, that they should be seen but not heard and that they should not be demanding or expressive of any negative emotions, can then learn that it can be more familiar to be the one who can offer support to others and can find themselves taking responsibility for everyone around them. They probably were not aware that a child should not feel familiar with the role of protector and primary supporter, and should have actually experienced repetitive protecting and supporting *from* the adults in their life. The child can grow up naturally taking on responsibility for their home, their adult who seemed to need them emotionally, alongside anyone else who may seem to need their attuned care and hoping for a sense of peace and calm. The child can learn to be naturally attuned to others' needs because they may have needed to learn to read the faces of their adults, in order to assess how to calm them or regulate them, in order to de-escalate any disaster or further distress. A child who does not repetitively experience their adult protecting them doesn't know that it is not appropriate for them as children to be relied upon emotionally and so continues to care for everyone that is in their world. They can then become exhausted and struggle to understand how healthy boundaries can protect them from feeling the weight of the world on their shoulders.

> These children need to have repetitive experiences of being protected, feeling known and cared for with important details recognized. The parent can be intentional about helping the child recognize that the adult is able to adult well and the child can relax and play. This can take countless repetitions but don't give up!

Not feeling a sense of belonging

When the child experiences emotional neglect or they do not have an adult who can offer enough emotional connection and support, they can have a deep unmet need to be a part of something where they know they fully belong and can be celebrated. This deep need to belong and be known and accepted can lead to being easily recruited into different groups and gangs because, even if they may at first feel uncomfortable about what is being asked of them, the need to be accepted into a group seems greater, which can cause them to ignore that discomfort and do whatever it takes to feel a sense of belonging. As humans, we are dependent on needing to belong in order to feel alive and connected, and so people will often do whatever it takes to feel that profound feeling that they crave because of the lack of feeling of family in childhood. Sadly, there are adults who exploit children because they are aware of this deep human subconscious need to belong. As a society, we need to be more aware of the power of belonging and intentionally create spaces for people to feel fully included, empowered to have a voice and take up space and be championed and celebrated, seen and heard.

> If at all possible, try and prioritize finding a group where the child can excel and be celebrated as they grow up, where they feel like they are 'like the others' and able to experience a sense of belonging. Also, be intentional about photos of the child with loved ones being around the home and letting their personal objects take up space there too.

Not able to be self-regulated

We know that before a child can demonstrate self-regulation they need enough experiences of co-regulation with an adult who is patient and can enable that child to feel supported and explore what they are feeling. Self-regulation is an experience that is felt in the body, emotions, mind and nervous system and therefore is not a cognitive exercise. When a child hasn't had enough repetitive experiences of co-regulation from an adult, they may not be able to self-regulate and may be emotionally explosive, dysregulated, angry or aggressive or instead be withdrawn, silent, dissociative and avoid feelings that seem intolerable in order to stay alive. Both hyper-aroused or hypo-aroused coping mechanisms can lead to difficulty with relationships and playing with others – especially if losing a game or disappointment are a possible experience. All forms of natural conflict may be avoided. This can of course lead to distress, isolation and feelings of rejection and sadness.

We are aware that during any periods of time where isolation is encouraged for children, whether that is as a punishment given to children who are seen to be 'naughty' or when a pandemic causes people to withdraw from others for safety, the lack of relational practice available to learn to self-regulate in the face of big feelings of anger, injustice, disappointment or frustration causes there to be an increase in chaos or coping mechanisms developed. Perry and Szalavitz (2006) describes the possible outcomes of the lack of relationship opportunities before such a pandemic:

> Children who don't get consistent, physical affection or the chance to build loving bonds simply don't receive the patterned, repetitive stimulation necessary to properly build the systems in the brain that connect reward, pleasure and human-to-human inter-actions. (p.86)

These children need as many experiences of co-regulation as possible in order to become familiar with the feelings, the overwhelm and the repair. Different social settings can be facilitated; these should start off small and safe and can grow as confidence grows.

Being the scapegoat

A lack of emotional connection in childhood can lead to a sense of shame, which is defined as feeling like there is something wrong with you at the very core of who you are. This feeling of shame can impact behaviour and relationships. Some children can end up being blamed for things that happen around them even when they were nothing to do with it, and rather than being able to argue or defend themselves or be defended by another adult, they can silently seem to agree with the accusations. This can lead to self-hatred and confusion. They can learn to tolerate the feeling that some days they seem to be praised and the next day criticized. It can seem to them like whatever they do they can't seem to work out how to earn the love they want. They can be told that they are too quiet or too loud, too dramatic or too sensitive, too confident or too shy. They can seem to find themselves unprotected and feeling like they can't quite do anything right.

> When we know that the child is sensitive to self-blame, we can be intentional about using words and facial responses to reassure them that they are not to blame. A good aim would also be to help them grow in confidence to defend themselves.

Over-achieving or compliance to find acceptance

Some children learn to try and find acceptance, belonging and love by being as perfect as they can. They can learn to be people-pleasers so they can experience some connection and be celebrated. They can learn to achieve above and beyond that which is normal in order to feel that sense of approval that was missing from the eyes of their adults in their early developmental years. Work can be addictive and success can be like a drug that offers relief from the feelings of distress for a short while until there needs to be more relief found.

Compliance is one of the most frustrating symptoms of trauma and especially complex trauma, because the child can be so focused on avoiding rejection and being 'good' that they push down their negative feelings as far as they can in order to retain an image that they have decided is what is required. When children are compliant they can be seen as being extra good and feel like they have value to others. The fear that they hold internally is of being rejected, unwanted or not belonging. However, I have often said that a happy, well-rounded child is one who has a sparkle in their eye, is a little bit cheeky and can enjoy the relationships around them, rather than exhausting themselves being on their best behaviour to earn acceptance.

> These children need to learn to tolerate little bits of mess or little mistakes and experience the love, empathy and relaxed reaction of those around them. Slowly, as words can be used to describe how painful it can feel but how normal it can be to make mess and mistakes, they can grow in tolerance and ease.

Independent and self-sufficient

It can be a natural outcome of emotional neglect and unmet needs for the child to be independent and self-sufficient, so that the vulnerability of having needs is not so intolerable.

Children can grow up learning not to expect much from anyone else, but trying to stay invisible, hidden, not take up too much space and be independent and solve challenges themselves. The feeling of vulnerability of needing others can create a harsh determination to be more self-reliant, in order to avoid feeling powerless in a world that seems frightening and overwhelming. It can feel wise to keep everything internalized and secret to avoid further hurt or hope for connection.

> Here it is vital that the adults don't make the child feel stupid, silly or incapable but, whilst encouraging their independence, also help them accept little bits of help until it feels less painful for them because they can grow in trust that you won't misuse that power and shame, abuse or embarrass them.

Intimacy and sex

Children who have not experienced a reciprocal relationship with an adult of being known and knowing another, can seek such a feeling of intimacy. They can misunderstand what intimacy is due to most online information creating the sense that sex and intimacy are the same thing. Many children begin to explore sex because they are looking for emotional intimacy due to the feeling of isolation and abandonment from an early age. Sex, and the physical experience of being naked and being 'known' in that vulnerable state, can be addictive as an alternative to investing into an authentic relationship where sex can be as a result of emotional intimacy, trust and love. If the child has not experienced the powerful feeling of being physically and emotionally held and safe, then they can be unaware of what to look for. Authenticity in relationships can be a concept that seems complex and unfamiliar and requires a lot of emotional effort and energy. Boundaries can be an unfamiliar concept and can often be ignored which can lead to the emotionally neglected child being abused by others, due to their lack of relational experience.

Sometimes the option of being a parent can seem attractive to a teenager, as a way to be loved and needed by another human, only to find that the needs of the little one can be overwhelming when they have so much unmet need of their own.

The feeling of void and numbness in the very centre of a person can be due to a lack of emotional connection with another who demonstrates love and availability in childhood. The desire can be strong to be seen and heard, but little information is available for how to have that as the child grows in age. The child can be confused with the need to be away from the chaos, volatility and noise of those they are around and yet be afraid of the echo of silence when they are alone. They can confuse solitude and isolation and forget that to choose to be alone can be a positive healing experience and is different to being isolated where they can feel abandoned and rejected.

Needing attention

When a child has grown up without enough attention or with the experience of painful mis-attuned parenting, where the child is reminded of how little their parent really knows them, they can either shut down and withdraw or seek attention from other places and people. The child may display behaviours that are clingy, emotionally demonstrative, volatile, chaotic, impulsive, reactive, restless, over-excited or hyper-aroused and fidgety. The need for reciprocal, repetitive, attuned nurture is high and yet their tolerance for the intensity that it creates can feel overwhelming, which means that there needs to be regular opportunities for emotionally connecting experiences that slowly build up the tolerance and lessen the intense desperation to be seen, heard and noticed.

The child needs enough experiences of belonging and being known and celebrated for who they are to enable any other gangs and unhealthy groups to be less needed. The people around the child need to model authentic conversation and relationships where people speak honestly (although not too much or it will overwhelm them) about their feelings, needs and positive experiences.

'I seem to have spent my entire life avoiding anyone being angry at me and hoping I'm doing a good enough job to not be noticed.'

Tom, aged 22

Reflection points

- What coping mechanisms do you see as common in relationship dynamics with young children when the child hasn't had enough emotional connection with their adult?

- What behaviours or coping mechanisms do you see with teenagers when they haven't had enough emotional connection with an adult?

- What is it they are really needing and where could they find that sense of belonging and acceptance in your local area?

Chapter Four

THE IMPACT OF EMOTIONAL NEGLECT ON THE EMOTIONS

When a baby has had repetitive experiences of feeling big emotions without a responsive adult offering enough comfort, soothing and emotional connection, it can lead to deep feelings of overwhelm, anxiety, anger, sensitivity, turmoil, sadness and fear. We also know that when a child is able to feel safe enough to express and explore emotional reactions with their primary caregiver, they grow up unafraid of those reactions and with the benefit of language to explore and describe them. This not only helps them when they are in different situations where emotions may be overwhelming, but also gives them the language to express what they may need without any shame.

Part of feeling known as a human is the experience of expressing emotions and thoughts and having a person acknowledge them and validate them. When this doesn't happen as a repetitive experience in early childhood, the child may learn to push away feelings or find other ways of coping with the confusion of what to do.

If a child hasn't had enough experiences of co-regulation in their early years (where an adult is able to attune to them, soothe them and explore what it is they may be feeling or needing), they can still catch up and become self-regulated, but compared to the natural time frame of developmental growth and learning in this area that should occur in the first five years, it can take many, many more repetitions to enable the development to take place. The work that we do in our trauma recovery centres with neglected children has shown that giving them the warm, attuned, repetitive, relational experiences that they missed can help them catch up, but it takes a long time to essentially rewire the brain and nervous system.

We know that often the parent has been unable to connect emotionally with the child due to their own childhood experiences where they may have been unaware of their own emotions, or if they are fearful of their own emotions which then sadly caused challenges for them.

So, what impact does emotional neglect have on the area of emotions?

Emotional regulation

When a child didn't have enough co-regulation in their early years, they can struggle to self-regulate and this can lead to explosive expressions of emotions or becoming numb and shut down on the inside due to the fear and unknown nature of what they may be feeling. When a child feels isolated, disconnected and confused with friendship expectations because of their lack of experience of emotional connection, it can be harder for them to be able to regulate their negative emotions when their whole neurobiological system is wired to survive the fear and confusion of being vulnerable. If the parent told the child to 'get over it' or to 'just stop worrying' or was angry with the child expressing any emotion or ignored them, then it can be tough for a child to learn about their emotions.

Learning how to express and regulate emotions needs to be done in the context of healthy relationships, which can be difficult when the parent is uncomfortable with emotions, unless they are committed to beginning to learn, in order to help their child, in which case, there is hope for both the child and adult to be able to grow and learn and develop emotional capacity.

Anger and defensiveness

Anger is an emotion that is a very normal reaction to injustice, frustration or disappointment. It can be a natural reaction to feeling rejected, misunderstood, abandoned, confused and disconnected. It is often the outward expression of a deep and uncomfortable feeling of sadness or grief. Anger can be an immediate, automatic reaction to any sense of threat or terror, and the expression of it can sometimes seem to be disproportionate, because the feeling can be growing over time on the inside and can be easily triggered by a smaller experience. Anger can be an instinctive protective mechanism to keep people away from a person if they suddenly feel vulnerable and they are scared that they will be taken advantage of in that state. The child can feel angry if they feel that everyone is rejecting or mocking or avoiding or leaving them out of something where others seem to be invited. The feeling of anger is not wrong, but it needs to be expressed in a way that can be contained by a caring, attuned, empathetic adult who can witness the pain. This can stop it being destructive, and when it is expressed it can cause less inner turmoil. As the child grows into adolescence, if they haven't had enough opportunities to express and explore the reasons for the anger that they feel, it can become like fuel in the flames of the hormonal changes of puberty and create explosive levels of aggressive or defensive behaviours.

_____

'I somehow felt like everyone was dangerous and everyone wanted to "get me". It took me ages not to be defensive and overreact when anyone said anything to me that wasn't shallow chatting. It was just how I had always been.'

Philip, aged 17, who was emotionally neglected as a child
_____

Terror and powerlessness

Terror and powerlessness are the primary experiences of being traumatized and when they are felt repetitively as a baby, this can lead to coping mechanisms to survive the feelings that can be so life-threatening. Hyper-vigilance is the ability to scan the environment, the faces of others and sense atmospheres in order to be ready for any further threat to try and stay safe. It is a trauma symptom that is due to trying to survive and avoid further terror, with the child wanting to be able to be more ready for any further experiences of terror, so that there is less shock and the impact can be more controlled. This can cause the baby and child to struggle to easily relax because they stay ready for another crisis, which means that as the child grows, they may begin to grasp at ways to remain in control or avoid anything that may produce more terror. If they experience the comfort and predictable emotional availability from a parent when they feel frightened, they will eventually, with a lot of repetition, learn that they can find help from another person.

Dissociation

Some children have to repress their emotions due to the lack of freedom to experiment with expressing them and the potential danger to their lives if they take up any time or space. When a person has repressed emotions, it can cause them to feel unwell and feel constricted and they can feel a sense of deep-down terror about what may happen.

If the child is being hurt or let down by the adult whose role it is to protect, soothe and respond to them, they cannot physically leave them to stay away from the source of pain and so they have to adopt a survival skill which is to separate on an emotional and awareness level, which is called dissociation. The clever internal coping mechanism keeps children alive because they look like they are present in the room, whilst they are actually hiding on the inside to avoid further turmoil and pain in the relationship. Sometimes they may appear to be dazed, daydreamy or floaty, and at other times they may appear to present with different moods or ways of being, because they are splitting on the inside to be able to avoid further terror, pain and punishment. It can lead to internal chaos as the different 'parts' of the person react to different experiences in the way that seems least stressful or dangerous. The consequence is that the child learns to avoid feeling the turmoil or terror and instead has this instinctive, automatic, internal way to cope with the different potential threats but also stops being able to live freely and naturally, trusting and enjoying the new opportunities that life may offer. When a child has had to develop many different 'parts' of themselves to survive different frightening environments, they can develop dissociative identity disorder (DID), where the psyche has split into many different parts, all of which 'hold' different experiences, memories and ways of being.

The dissociative system is a coping mechanism that is often present when the child has experienced emotional neglect or unmet emotional needs and they have had to find ways of coping without trusting an adult for protection and guidance. Depersonalization is the ability to not feel the physical feelings such as hunger, anger, deep sadness or turmoil or the body pains that occur due to physical or sexual abuse. But although depersonalization is a clever coping mechanism in the heat of the terror, it can be difficult to then notice any warning signs that the body may be able to offer outside of the trauma, such as burning themselves, hunger, thirst, terror or sadness and instead they become separated from those life-giving and helpful feelings.

Derealization is the coping mechanism that often follows emotional neglect as it enables a child to stay physically present but be emotionally away, and in their mind be in another space that feels safer, where they have control and a sense of safety. The child may look like they are 'in their own world' and look like they are daydreaming, but the world where 'they go' can feel far more real than the place they are sitting due to the need to locate themselves in their imagination in order to survive. (You can read more about dissociation in *The Simple Guide to Complex Trauma and Dissociation* (de Thierry 2020)).

Depression or feeling tired

When a child is carrying unmet needs, inner turmoil, sadness, grief, confusion and frustration, they can feel physically tired and exhausted. Lethargy is a natural consequence of feeling overwhelmed and wanting to withdraw and hide from the world that can seem to be so frightening.

When the child hasn't got a safe adult with whom to explore their internal reactions and feelings, they can feel overwhelmed, exhausted and sad. Sometimes they may then quickly escalate into an opposite survival mechanism which is where the feeling of tiredness and overwhelm is so scary that they need to have power, control and energy. When this 'switch' into hyper-arousal is activated, adrenaline and cortisol can be released and they can become defensive and full of survival energy. Some children spend longer in hypo-arousal where lethargy and overwhelm are dominant and others spend longer in hyper-arousal where they are fighting to stay alive and others switch between the two all the time.

Some children live with a constant feeling of sadness which they try to cope with through addictions or other soothing, numbing behaviours that lower the feeling of pain. The sadness can feel like a heavy coat that just sits on them and stops life being fun and an adventure, because their primary aim is to survive. Some children live with anxiety as the tip of the iceberg of the terror that they have buried on their insides. They can try and avoid doing anything that could cause further pain, terror, rejection, abandonment, sadness or shame, which leads to only experiencing some of life and missing out on risk and adventure.

What the child needs is space to be seen and heard and where their emotions can be explored, expressed and validated, including the big feelings of sadness that can feel far too huge to even contemplate expressing in a safe way.

Shame

Shame is a consequence of trauma and causes the child to believe that whatever is happening is probably their fault and because they are 'bad'. Guilt is different because the person can attempt to fix or apologize for what has happened. In the book, *The Simple Guide to Understanding Shame*, I give an explanation of the impact of the experience of shame: 'Shame is an extraordinarily powerful, instinctive, primitive feeling and bodily experience that overwhelms a person. People who experience shame will instinctively find ways of avoiding the intensity of this feeling' (de Thierry 2019, p.19).

Shame is a person's feeling of being in the core of who they are, where they feel that they are not wanted, rejected, a failure and damaged. Shame can cause different coping mechanisms to be used in order to avoid feeling the awful feeling, but these often lead to further disconnection from others rather than a sense of belonging. Shame is a natural consequence of experiencing emotional unmet needs, because the child believes that they must be too awful to get to know. Shame loses its power when it can be spoken about, acknowledged and the shame thoughts can be seen as not true.

The emotions of a child are deeply impacted by emotional neglect and unmet emotional needs, and they can hold back the child and the adult they become from being able to throw themselves fully into a dynamic life full of adventure and challenge. In the context of a nurturing parent or a kind secondary attachment figure, they can begin to notice, acknowledge, feel and have validated these emotions until they lose their overwhelming feeling.

Reflection points

- What dominant emotions have you witnessed in a child who has been neglected or had unmet needs?

- What coping mechanisms have they used to cope with these big feelings?

- What is it that they need from us adults to feel the emotions again and feel safe?

Chapter Five

THE IMPACT ON THE
BODY AND BRAIN

As we have been exploring so far in this book, we know that a baby, and then child, needs at least one attachment relationship or primary caregiver where they experience being soothed, cared for and nurtured repetitively in order to develop in a healthy way. When a child has relationships where they feel safe and happy, they have natural opportunities for playful, fun and purposed movement that helps to strengthen and develop different areas of the body and sensory systems that enable healthy growth. When this has been a consistent experience, the child is able to develop in a healthy way, which is the foundation from which to explore the world, communicate with others and learn how to ask for help when they need it.

We know that when a child experiences emotional neglect or unmet emotional needs, they have often not had enough repetitive nurture that was felt in their body and is associated with the powerful and attuned attention of an adult. This chapter explores what the impact of that could be.

The impact of touch

One of the best ways to communicate care, nurture and attention to a baby is through touch. The holding, rocking, swaying, stroking and attentive connection builds the baby's brain. This kind of soothing touch is essential for healthy development of a baby who can respond to the touch by relaxing in the care of the caregiver. Whilst this book is not about physical neglect, we recognize that where there is emotional neglect or unmet emotional needs, there can be less touch and less physical play in the early years that can lead to developmental delays and difficulties that interfere with positive growth.

Positive touch and soothing is important to help a child learn what it is to be a human who feels and has skin that can enjoy the feeling of touch from a safe and caring person. Touch helps the growth of the nervous system and decreases stress hormones. It makes us feel loved, connected and alive. When a child didn't have enough touch in a natural, warm, positive, emotionally connecting, natural way, they can feel trapped in their own bodies and be rigid or floaty. This positive touch needs to be a natural part of the parenting and caring of a baby which leads to the healthy growth of the nervous system and decreases stress. Oxytocin is a hormone that is naturally released when someone feels a positive connection with another person and it can act as a pain relief and can dispel a sense of fear. In fact, research shows that 'elevated levels of oxytocin are associated with increased trust, cooperative behaviour, sharing with strangers, the more effective reading of others' emotions; and more constructive resolution' (Gorney 2022, p.48).

Positive nurturing touch helps the child to feel fully alive in their body and connected to another human who can protect and nurture them. That makes them relax into the feeling of safety.

When a child hasn't been regularly stroked, held with soothing sounds and movements and experienced the positive feeling of being looked at with eyes full of love, the child can feel frightened and overwhelmed by the world. They can feel unprotected and abandoned on a deep primitive level, which can hinder healthy growth and it can cause them to feel trapped inside a body that doesn't feel familiar. They can grow up feeling psychologically untouchable and like there is something wrong with them at a core level. We know that the earlier the touch deprivation, the more the negative impact increases.

If, however, the child feels soothing and nurturing touch whilst simultaneously seeing the adult's face looking angry or distanced, then the touch can lead to fear. The mismatch of the touch being potentially positive but the face or nervous system being negative or disengaged can lead to internal stress and increased fear of what is happening. If the adult is holding the child but is dissociative or angry or frustrated, the touch can cause the child to breathe in a shallow way and hold themselves back from any expression that could be sensed as life-threatening in that moment.

Most hospitals now recognize the power of the parents' touch and encourage skin-to-skin experiences as soon as possible after birth, so that the baby feels safe and 'held'. In fact:

A recent study co-ordinated by the World Health Organization at Safdarjung and four other hospitals found that kangaroo care [where an adult holds the baby skin to skin on their chest] is even more effective when it is continuous and starts immediately after birth, rather than for a few hours a day after the baby is judged stable. Researchers estimate this approach could save 150,000 lives a year. (Gorney 2022, p.41)

We know that when a baby or a child is left physically on their own for any length of time it can be deeply stressful. This is different from a child choosing to withdraw and be on their own, where they feel in control. Children need to feel connected to and near an adult who can help them so that they don't feel powerless and frightened. They should experience being rocked, thrown in the air with laughter, patted and massaged in age-appropriate ways and as they get older only with consent that is authentic. This helps them feel like they own their own body and they can feel familiar in their own skin, rather than feel like a stranger to themselves.

When a child hasn't had enough touch and playful interactions with their body such as rocking, jumping, swinging and other such large movements they can end up with behaviours that involve tense shoulders, holding their breath, exhaustion from holding things in, avoidance of hugs and avoidance of any other touch, which can lead to isolation and fear of connection and digestive issues from the tension. It's never too late to start to explore different soothing touch and large movement activities; as long as the child can feel 100 per cent able to say 'no' to anything that makes them feel uncomfortable.

'When I got to being 15 all my friends started hugging but I didn't know how to, so I got a pillow out and practised at home. I didn't know that my friends grew up with hugs.'

Julia, aged 28

Sensory sensitivity

When a child has experienced emotionally connected and attuned parenting, they are able to feel at home in their own body. They feel in control and comfortable being around other people and keeping the boundary of their body. When a child has not had that repetitive nurturing touch and soothing, they can feel shocked and unsettled if someone brushes past them, or if someone touches their shoulder. Their body can become rigid or shut down in order to avoid processing the feelings that the touch can elicit. They may have the automatic experience of depersonalization where they have stopped feeling aspects of their body due to past traumatic experiences where they felt intolerable pain. Depersonalization is a clever coping mechanism that enables a child or adult to stay alive when the pain that they feel, whether it is from hunger or abuse, is too intolerable. This can become a normal state for some people who have experienced trauma in their body or not enough careful, attuned nurture using touch and movement.

In their book about empathy, Szalavitz and Perry (2010) describe how a girl who grew up in an orphanage describes her sensory challenges following emotional neglect. She describes how she now doesn't like being touched as an adult. She speaks about how the impact of her lack of being held as a baby has:

> …made physical contact unfamiliar, novel, and, therefore, anxiety provoking, rather than pleasurable – it's something she has to control if she is to feel safe. She also has sensory differences. She needs absolute dark to sleep, finds bright lights bothersome, and, as a child needed to wear only soft fabrics because other clothing was unbearable. (Szalavitz & Perry 2010, p.70)

When a child experiences playful touching, such as the throwing of the baby in the air, rocking back and forth or twirling around the legs of the adult, they are activating the vestibular system that enables the child to grow in subconscious knowledge of how they fit into the space around them. The vestibular system, which is the first sensory system to develop in the womb, is really important for everyday life because it controls a lot of the brain's information processing that helps with having enough core stability to move, have good balance and posture, alongside other sensory information that is received via other senses; it also helps with body awareness and motion perception, which can lead to more natural behaviour impulse control. Children and adults of all ages can find important benefits in exploring different sensory experiences and what impact they have, with the aim of finding different movements and sensory stimuli that can bring comfort, safety and feelings of being alive or connected to their own body.

Movement

When a child has been emotionally neglected in their early years they may need to have opportunities to develop and strengthen the three main sensory systems that didn't have enough positive experiences in a playful relationship with their parents. The vestibular system, as mentioned, is important for core stability; the tactile system is vital for helping the child understand different sensations, like taste and touch; and the proprioceptive system is about body awareness. It is important to recognize the negative impact on so many areas of development of 'not enough' movement and playful exploration, particularly in the sensitive period of growth in the early years, and simultaneously recognize the ability for recovery and catching up if time and attention are given. A trauma-informed occupational therapist can do a thorough assessment of these areas that need strengthening and then help them develop through exercises that are seen by the children as fun games and time for building connection together with a parent.

Food and eating

Food can be an area of intense emotion due to the lack of positive association of food with nurture and connection. Eating can either feel desperate and scary, or desperate and full of excitement and energy, or it can feel mostly like a source of fear and confusion. This can lead to avoidance or control or emotional outbursts about the smallest irritations from timing, portion size, shape, texture, smell, packaging or any other aspect that is not what they had expected. When a baby and child experiences feeding as a time of nurture, emotional connection and playfulness, they are more likely to have strong oral motor strength that allows them to chew, enjoy various textures of food and speak easily. When that hasn't happened, food needs to be offered in ways that are mindful to the lack of positive nurturing experience and now incorporates fun, relaxed exploration and a knowledge that it is an area of low strength that needs focus to develop it, in the context of a warm and fun relationship.

Dissociation

When a child's needs aren't met by the parent, the child can be left feeling intolerable turmoil and inner chaos as they are left muddled about who they are, what is wrong with them, why they don't feel loved and why they feel rejected. This can lead to the coping mechanism of dissociation where they either have to separate off from their emotions so they don't have to feel them, or they separate off from their body sensations so they don't have to feel the pain and turmoil that can be felt in their chest or stomach or head. This is explored in other chapters and in my book, *The Simple Guide to Complex Trauma and Dissociation* (2020).

Stress for a baby

Stress is something that a baby should only experience for short bursts until they feel the powerful relief of soothing and comfort that stops the frightening feeling. Stress is a state of high arousal that is full of fear and terror to a baby or child, who is powerless and dependent on the adult for protection. A baby can experience stress in the womb, in the birth experience, in the first days, weeks and months of life and this can have an impact on their healthy development unless there is intentional soothing and calming offered to the little one. Gerhardt (2004) explains that:

> …the baby's vulnerability to mishandling can start even earlier, in the womb. Even at this stage, it is the elements of the brain responsible for responding to stress which are amongst the most vulnerable parts of the brain. As early as pregnancy, the stress response is already forming within the developing foetus and can be affected by the mother's state of health. In particular, her high cortisol could pass through the placenta into his brain (Gitau *et al.* 2021a) potentially affecting his hypothalamus and hippocampus. (p.67)

Cortisol, which is the automatic response to feelings of stress, can be released into the bloodstream of the child and, in large quantities, this can be damaging because when it is generated in a crisis, it can essentially 'put on hold' other bodily functions. A child being around a parent who is stressed can cause cortisol to rise in them, as both of them become alert for danger and try to focus on surviving the stressor. There are different ways to reduce cortisol, such as outside walks, breathing exercises, gentle exercise, bilateral stimulation such as marching and clapping, soothing smells and textures. Exploring these methods is vital for a reduction in stress activation.

Addiction

We know that when a child is left with unmet emotional needs, there are many coping mechanisms that can be created automatically and instinctively to help them stay alive in the face of feeling such turmoil and adversity. Despite the sophistication of the internal coping mechanisms that tend to become normal for them, the child or adult can still feel a deep sense of turmoil or inner discomfort or lack of ease and this could cause them to turn towards further methods of trying to numb and not experience these distracting and painful feelings. When someone is looking for a method of soothing, there are usually lots of messages in our society that indicate that different activities can numb and dull the pain felt internally. They can be healthy activities that can become addictive due to the positive feelings released following the experience – such as exercise, eating food or achieving success – or they can be drugs or alcohol that are so readily available to anyone who needs additional support, which can be addictive and destructive to the body and brain of the person needing the help. We recognize that many traumatized people end up in different addictive behaviours due to the overwhelming feelings of pain and turmoil that can somehow feel out of control, endless, life debilitating and life destroying. If the traumatic experience is emotional neglect, which comes with so few words that can adequately describe the level of distress, the addictions can seem to be separated from the root cause of distress and can even lead to the person feeling shame that they are struggling to 'cope' with the demands of life. All addiction is due to the pain and turmoil of trauma that often cannot be put into words and the escalated stress on the body is immense and deeply unfair. The main alternative is to introduce to the child methods of expressing the negative feelings that are brewing on the inside of them, before they feel even more overwhelming. As they grow in courage to explore these difficult sensations and feelings, they will not seek out popular numbing mechanisms so urgently. Investing into helping them to explore their difficult feelings is vital before puberty if at all possible, because the possibility of being offered alternative coping mechanisms is very high after that!

Hypervigilance

When a child needs to be alert for danger, both in their surroundings but also when they see the face of their parent looking angry or frustrated, they can then begin to learn hypervigilance. This is another automatic coping mechanism that enables the child to scan constantly, looking for signs of danger that can warn them ahead of time how to stay safe and alive. They can notice the smallest change of facial reaction or raised eyebrow or slight change of a tone of voice, and can react in ways that again may seem disproportionate. The attunement that they so wanted as a child from their parent is now a skill they utilize to stay safe. They can 'read' another person's nervous system and from that decide if they feel safe or not. To stay in a state of hypervigilance is exhausting, which can lead to the child preferring to stay in smaller, controlled places such as their room, where they can limit the need to scan for danger all the time. The child needs to have the choice to have time spent in environments that feel smaller and less overwhelming, so that they can lower their heightened state of alert for danger and threat.

Challenges in communication

When a child has been neglected, it not only impacts the child's confidence in relationships, emotional regulation and behaviour, it also causes neurobiological change to an important function in the brain. The corpus callosum is responsible for communication between the two hemispheres of the brain and more efficient learning and recall for both verbal and visual information.

In a study, the corpus callosum was found to be 15–18 per cent smaller in brains of children who had been neglected (Teicher *et al.* 2014). This informs us that language comprehension, humour, social reasoning, and recognition of facial expression can be harder to comprehend when a child is neglected. Often, when we may not know that they have not had enough emotional connection in their early years, which has caused the lack of ease in areas of relationship and emotion, children are accused of not trying hard enough. To strengthen the corpus callosum, children need to do as many bilateral stimulating exercises as possible, whilst using stories and metaphors to help them explore how they feel, because this uses both hemispheres of the brain which then strengthens the corpus callosum.

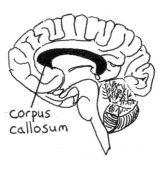

corpus
callosum

Conclusion

Whilst we know that the impact of negative touch can be devastating and the impact of 'not enough' positive touch can be equally disastrous for the developing brain and body of the child, we also know that the more positive experiences we can provide for a child or young person, the more likely they are to have some repair from the early damage. There are lots of exercises and activities that can be done in playful, fun, emotionally connecting ways, which enable the body to be soothed and be able to release and express some of the trapped pain and turmoil.

Reflection points

- What kind of touch did you feel was positive when you were little?

- What reactions to movement, spatial awareness and their own body have you seen from children who have not had 'enough' positive touch?

- What kind of activities or games are you facilitating that can repair some of the lack of experience that a child has had?

Chapter Six

THE IMPACT ON THE SENSE OF SELF AND IDENTITY

The impact of emotional neglect or unmet emotional need can be seen on many levels, including relationships, emotions, the body, brain and the child's sense of self.

The child's sense of self is their identity: their ability to be sure of themselves, who they are, where they come from and how they fit into the world. When they have a confident sense of self, they generally grow into self-assured people who are able to contribute to the world with the gifts and talents that they know they have and with a healthy self-awareness of their weaknesses. The lack of a sense of self can also cause low self-esteem or self-loathing.

Voicelessness

When a child does not have enough emotional connection and repetitive experiences where they feel known, loved, understood, seen, heard and able to explore their emotions, they can end up feeling confused and uncertain about how to connect with others. They can lack confidence in their ability to put into words how they feel, what is going on and can consequently end up talking with others about non-personal matters such as world issues rather than themselves, their reactions and place in the world. This can lead them to further lose the ability to grow in confidence in connecting emotionally, being confident speaking, wondering out loud, feeling listened to and knowing that their opinions are valued. The lack of confidence in communicating with others can lead to further internalization which can cause emotions and confusions to be stuck on the inside. They can miss out on the opportunities to be around others who would be able to offer the opportunity to help them process and make sense of their thoughts, worries and muddles. This can then lead them to feel voiceless, which then in turn can cause them to strengthen their negative internal beliefs about wanting to be alone, and not wanting to join in with others in discussion or chats, which can then further lead to loneliness and isolation.

A child first 'finds themselves' in the interactions of their primary caregiver, their facial responses, body warmth and loving reciprocal exchanges. The child sees in their parent's eyes the look of love, care and pleasure and they then know they are loved, cared for and a source of delight and pleasure. That is the very beginning of their sense of self developing. The journey of development continues as the baby interacts with the primary caregiver(s) and continues to enjoy working out how to get different reactions from them; and in that early context they can begin to work out what behaviour is most celebrated and delighted in. They can then enjoy repeating those movements, facial reactions or reactions in a delighted performance, eager to experience the reciprocal squeals of delight from the primary caregiver! These repetitive interactions demonstrate behaviour of a child with secure attachment and it's that foundation that 'permits the development of a self-identity as a person worthy of love and care and a capacity to love and care for others' (Herman 1994, p.261).

It is also worth noting that when a child's home life is confusing, they may lie to defend it and to give a more socially accepted reason for their behaviour or emotions. Lying is always a sign of fear or defensiveness and we should be curious if we think there may be lying, so that we can help the child explore how they really feel.

Social context

We know that the human brain is dependent on a social context for healthy development. The child first needs the primary attachment figures and then other social experiences in order to find their place in the world. These interactions with others teach the child how they fit in and what the unwritten rules of socialization are. The child is unable to develop a sense of self without developing a felt sense of others in repetitive interactions that shape the nervous system and create an understanding of the world and the child's place within it. It is often not an easy journey being a human, with frequent feelings of fear, powerlessness and shame arising, which makes it difficult to learn the art of relationships, especially when so many social settings have invisible, unwritten social expectations. Perry affirms the complexity of socialization by explaining that:

> …humans evolved to be especially sensitive to social cues. In fact, the complexity of dealing with group social life is believed to be one of the key reasons our brains became so big. But like so many characteristics of the human brain, this sensitivity is a double-edged sword. It allows us to

adapt to varying social conditions – but the adaptations that are helpful in one set of circumstances can be outright harmful in another. (Szalavitz & Perry 2010, p.104)

Not knowing what you are good at

When the child doesn't have regular, repetitive, specific, positive affirmation from their parents, either because they are not physically or emotionally present or because the parent fears that they may become arrogant and undermine their authority, the child can be left not knowing what their strengths and weaknesses are. This can lead them to feeling a lack of vision or hope for the future as they try and work out what they are skilled at and where they fit in the world. A part of someone's sense of identity lies in knowing what they enjoy doing, what they seem to have some success in and how they then feel about that. Often children show some early interest in some areas that develop into a strength and skill and whilst attuned parents can notice that and help them grow in confidence in those areas, a child who is emotionally neglected is in survival mode and the parents are often not able to notice these small signs of interest or skill. Sadly, when the adults' emotional needs take up more airspace than the child's, they may not be able to notice when the child needs any emotional support and that can lead the child to feel isolated and misunderstood.

The mess of the inner self

When a child has been focusing on trying to survive without the emotional support of a parent, they can often end up feeling that they have a volcano on their insides which could start to rumble or explode at any time. The volcano is a mixture of unexpressed feelings, pain and turmoil, alongside physical pains and memories of when they reacted in ways they didn't mean to, and relationship disappointment where they didn't grasp some of the complexities of the social expectations. This can feel like a heavy weight of pain and hurt and can cause them to feel ashamed and want to hide how they really feel and put on an outward show of being frightening instead. Sometimes it seems easier to act defensively and push people away than let anyone near you, in case they also hurt you. Many children and young people hope that we as adults can see the frightened little child on the inside of their harder 'outer shell' that can swear and be angry to keep people at a distance.

We once had a profound moment when three very distressed adolescent girls that we were helping at one of our centres started to gently turn over all the furniture in a therapy space, and then proceeded to rip up about five toilet rolls and scatter the paper all over the furniture. As a psychotherapist and team of mentors, we were fascinated and didn't stop them but expressed our curiosity. They kept checking our faces and then after what seemed like quite a while, they seemed to finish and proclaimed they were done. It felt like they were constantly checking to see whether we would be angry, upset or frustrated with the mess. We weren't at all, because we were completely curious, and it felt like behaviour from toddlers who were testing our boundaries. We eventually asked if we should help them pop everything back, and they smiled and looked intently at us and we spent a fun 20 minutes together with the girls, collecting the toilet paper and returning the furniture to the right places. Although they tried to look wild and carefree as they made the mess, they were studying our faces to see how we would react and once they saw that we could 'contain their mess' and help them in the restoration of the room, they seemed more able to trust us with their own inner feelings of mess and upturned lives, knowing that we would work with them to support them in the restoration process. Often young people and children will speak in 'the metaphor' because they would find words too painful to use.

'I would describe myself as a chameleon as I was just who I needed to be in whatever place I was. I was never the same as I didn't know who I really was. I just changed to fit in and not be noticed.'

Romy, aged 40

Feelings of low self-esteem

Children who don't feel seen and heard can develop feelings of rejection and not being wanted and that their voice and opinion is not worth anything. Children need to experience the joy of being delighted in when they are little, with big movements and expressions, in order for them to grow a healthy self-esteem and, as they grow older, to feel able to relax in the safe knowledge that they are loved, valued, unique and wanted. When this isn't communicated effectively, the child can end up feeling lost and looking for a sense of worth in achievement, in friendships, in being perfect and in pleasing others, or they can shut down, withdraw and go through life in autopilot.

A low self-esteem tends to 'leak' out of people with words and comments that demonstrate that they don't feel pleased with themselves. They can speak with angry, self-deprecating comments that they may have heard others say to them. They can avoid trying hard in case they prove to themselves that they are as useless as they feel. They may avoid speaking or doing anything in public for the same reason. Words of encouragement or affirmation need to be specific or they will bounce off a child who will assume that they are spoken to everyone. General encouragement will be often ignored as they will assume that it is not directed at them.

They can feel very small and invisible and unseen and so feel bad about themselves and blame themselves for everything around them that goes wrong. The answer to restoring damaged self-esteem is long-term, repetitive, specific encouragement and expressed delight to have the child around. A traumatized child can also spot a fake comment and will be looking, in a hypervigilant way, for signs of authentic care and approval. In fact, if a parent says 'I love you' but doesn't spend time being emotionally available and co-regulating, it can be confusing for the child.

How to help a child develop a healthy sense of self

Children develop a healthy sense of self by having adults see them doing well at something, or see their unique fascination with something, or when they seem to enjoy or are fascinated by something and they reflect back to them. This gentle attuned reflection enables the child to be continually curious about what it feels like to be them in different places. The kind of areas that they need naturally reflected back with attuned conversation that is not too intense include:

- what they are good at

- what they are not as good at

- what they dream of

- what makes them happy

- what has gone wrong

- what has gone well

- who loves them

- who they love.

When these things become clear and are naturally allowed to be forever updated as they get older, and they can see them visually represented in the home in photos and pictures, they can grasp an internal sense of self and how they fit into the world and they can have the language to confidently announce things like, 'I used to really like dolls but now I enjoy designing clothes' or 'I used to find writing difficult but now I think I'm quite good at it'. These verbalized sentences, in the context of a healthy, emotionally connected relationship, demonstrate that the child is able to go on the continual journey of self-discovery where they feel that there is room to change their mind and explore who they are and where they fit in the world.

Reflection points

- How can emotional neglect impact the child's sense of self?

- How can the child find themselves and how they fit in the world?

- What can be a hindrance to them developing a strong sense of self?

Chapter Seven

WHAT DOES THE RECOVERY JOURNEY LOOK LIKE?

Recovery is possible and the younger the child is when they begin the journey of recovery, the less time and intensity it can take. Recovery is still possible in adulthood, but it takes significantly longer and requires potentially more patience from the relationships that are supporting the emotionally traumatized person.

Psychoeducation and modelling externalization

The recovery journey begins with psychoeducation. When the adult can understand more of what is going on and why, they feel less powerless when behaviour and emotions can be explosive, and instead feel more empowered to help. When the child can begin to understand some of what is going on and have language to use about how their 'insides' feel sadness, fear or hurt, they can also begin to grow in curiosity. Curiosity enables them to reflect and wonder what is going on, rather than react with shame and self-hatred for being a 'bad person'.

Adults need to come up with the most creative ways to explain about the power of emotions, the need to express them, the power of words and need to express ourselves and what it is like to be a human. When the learning can be undertaken with play and fun and emotional connectedness, the child begins to grasp more of a sense of what is happening and has language to describe it. There are videos, films, games and art activities that can be used to help the child begin to explore their feelings. If the child hears the caring adults talk about how some feelings can be hard and how some body sensations can be muddled, they can feel less shame about their own confusion. Shame stops curiosity and reflection and causes defensive behaviour that protects the fragile sense of self, and so conversation and play about psychoeducation needs to be overtly aimed at decreasing the power of shame with natural fun and modelling.

> Oh! Mummy is just wondering if she needs a drink or a snack?

> I am wondering if I am tired and need a rest or I need to run a little bit and wake myself up as I have been sitting for too long!

When a child grows up hearing these kinds of gentle reflections modelled, they can learn to adopt a similar approach and externalize verbally some of their internal muddles, which then enable the adult to help navigate them through the maze of emotions, feelings and sensations that may be sending multiple internal messages that overwhelm the child.

Understanding what is going on and why is halfway through to recovery, which is why over half of this book is taken up with psychoeducation. When we understand ourselves, we can feel more relaxed and less frustrated with ourselves.

Relationships and trust

We know that when a person has been hurt in a relationship they need to heal through a relationship, and so a vital part of the recovery journey is enough positive relational experiences being offered to the child. When the child has several different repetitive, positive experiences of feeling safe, belonging and being seen and heard, they can begin to grow stronger in areas that have had less experience. The key areas of relationship that need to be offered to the child who has had some traumatic experiences of not enough emotional connection are attunement, validation, containment and soothing.

The child needs the adult to be attuned to how they may be feeling and gently express that in words:

> I wonder if today you are feeling unsure about this activity because you didn't enjoy lunch, so I wonder if you are feeling a little sad...

These gentle reflections can help a child hear that the adult has noticed that they struggled with that lunch option and that it may impact on their mood, which could cause them to feel less able to take a risk with the activity. When this kind of reflection is offered repetitively, the child can also learn the way different experiences can bring influence and use words to describe it and then ask for help.

Validation is about acknowledging that the emotion or sensation is a felt experience – even if it doesn't make much sense. When a person feels validated, they are then able to reflect and sometimes change their mind about what they are feeling, but if they are fighting to have the warm and relieving feeling of being seen and validated, then they could remain stubborn and assert their rights rather than gently lean in to acknowledge their feelings. It's not about logic and being 'right', but about being heard and seen and listened to.

Containment is also an essential experience for a child. When a child feels out of control, with powerful emotions that can seem frightening to them, and body sensations that can also feel overwhelming, they need the experience of being contained and held emotionally by someone who is not afraid or overwhelmed by the feelings, emotions and behaviour, but can remain calm and confident in the face of the chaos. When a baby feels this, they feel safe within what feels like the enormous soft and warm body of the strong adult. When a baby hasn't had that feeling enough, they can feel like they are not safe and will notice when adults who are meant to be looking after them show facial reactions and body movements that indicate that they are frightened too. This can then escalate the feelings of terror because they suddenly feel so small, but also so powerful and too scary to be looked after and loved. When an adult can emotionally contain and hold the child's feelings, they feel safe, calm and can soon de-escalate from their strong feelings of fear and instead rest in the arms or company of the adult who is calm and trying to bring comfort.

Babies need cuddles and rocking; toddlers need sensory transitional objects that smell and feel familiar and safe; children need sensory objects that quickly bring a sense of comfort, alongside the face, tone of voice and words of the adult who is able to speak kind words of safety. The rhythmic, melodic tone of voice of the caring adult can be as helpful as the content of the words. Smells that are associated with a kind person or a safe space can be quickly used to bring a sense of calm because the smell centre of the brain – the primary olfactory cortex – is next to the amygdala which is responsible for emotions such as fear in the brain, and so the calm smell can quickly calm the sense of fear.

With repetitive, positive, warm, kind nurturing attuned relational interactions, the child can slowly recover from the lonely, sad, distressing emotional pain that they have endured.

Changing self-neglect into self-nurture

When a child has felt unloved and not known, they can reject themselves before more people seem to reject them. If they haven't had attention paid to their needs, it can be an alien concept to them to nurture themselves and so they need to be shown how to, by teaching them habits that they can use that nurture their body, their emotions and their fragility. They can also find themselves at ease with self-hatred, which is a coping mechanism that can be used to try and protect them by helping them feel more in control in the face of potentially painful relationships. The child can learn to view all mistakes and imperfection as confirmation that they are 'useless' and not deserving of love. Whilst it can take time to change the self-talk to become positive, the child can be taught how to take care of and nurture different aspects of themselves. They can be introduced to smells, different sensory comforts and tastes and routines that can be nurturing. Slowly they can enjoy these things and seek them out to bring comfort to themselves. These different sensory experiences are important for the child to explore before adolescence if possible, when less positive, addictive behaviours are suggested to be comforting, soothing, exhilarating or exciting.

When a child hears repetitive words of encouragement and kindness, they can begin to take them on in their internal self-talk and they can learn to speak affirmatively to themselves. So even if they look like they are not listening, they usually are!

Noticing negative core beliefs

It's important to help a child begin to be curious about internal negative self-beliefs so that they can spot them, externalize them and be curious about how they got there, in order to wonder if another belief could be adopted instead.

'I am stupid and can't do this work.'

'I saw some brilliant writing that you did yesterday and I don't think you are stupid but that you are actually clever and good at writing and can have a good go at this maths.'

When an adult can help support the child emotionally with the reflections around core beliefs, we can see them gain confidence in speaking them aloud, which gives the possibility of change. When they stay inside, in the secret silence of the child's ponderings about the world, they can become deeply felt, and grow in toxicity. That does require us as the adults not to be too angry, frustrated and quick to say how mad the negative self-belief is, but to express sadness gently, and to offer an alternative belief that can be thought about as an option. The more mocking, teasing, cruel and nasty words have been spoken to the child, the gentler and more repetitive we have to be to see change happen.

'I realized that I just thought I was stupid. No one had told me I could learn and could do anything good really! Once I realized that there was a possibility of being OK at something I tried for the first time. I was 15!'

Samba, aged 19

Noticing the body sensations and movement

When the child has body sensations (such as feeling their tummy when they are hungry or feeling the tears well up in their eyes) that they may be unfamiliar with, it can be the instinctive reaction to push them down, try not to feel them and ignore them. We know that depersonalization, the subconscious coping mechanism of not feeling their body sensations, or derealization, when they are not emotionally present in day-to-day moments, can be very helpful for them to survive so many difficult and challenging feelings and thoughts and worries. Therefore, we don't want to immediately suggest that they are not needed, but we can help the child to be brave enough to feel a little feeling at a time and tolerate it. It can be best to help the child focus on a little sensation first that is not scary, such as the feeling of the tanginess of an orange slice. As they grow in fascination with what that feels like, they can explore some other tastes and body sensations. This can be a good foundation for tolerating less pleasant sensations that they can then reflect on, so that they can be more in control of what they do and don't like in relation to their body. We know that if they feel any negative, distressing or frightening sensation for too much time, it could cause deep distress and trigger early feelings of being alone and terrified with no comfort and so this needs a careful, gentle, curious approach. One other subconscious way that a child can avoid feelings, both emotions and body sensations, is to keep moving in a hyperactive way, where they feel the adrenaline causing them to feel alive but they don't have to face and 'feel' the troubling or uncomfortable feelings that may remind them of past experiences or pains. This can cause them to be hyperactive and cause them to find it difficult to settle to learn, think or play quietly.

Exploring safety

Helping a child explore what safety is is an essential part of the recovery journey. Safety is mostly about the 'who' in their world that has spent time building an emotionally connected relationship where the child experiences that relief of a strong adult who can contain, validate and soothe the child. That relationship can act as a foundation for the child to then find sensory reminders of that feeling of safety, such as things that they can smell, touch and be with that help them feel that warm, cosy, comfy feeling where they are less hypervigilant and anxious. They can grow in their knowledge of what safety is and what it feels like as they begin to know themselves more.

Conclusion

Recovery is ultimately about learning to feel safe in your own skin and experience felt safety in your body, emotions and relationships. It's about relational connection to others and a feeling of belonging and sense of self. In the words of van der Kolk, 'the challenge of recovery is to re-establish ownership of your body, your mind, your self' (2014, p.103).

Reflection points

- What can I do as an adult trying to offer a positive relationship to help someone heal from emotional unmet needs?

- How do I feel about modelling externalization to help release a child from the confusion of internalization and disconnection?

- What self-care tips can I introduce that are age-appropriate for the child to begin to explore soothing and felt safety?

Chapter Eight

ACTIVITIES TO HELP AN EMOTIONALLY NEGLECTED CHILD HEAL

When the parent and/or another attachment figure (class-room assistant/mentor/therapist) can understand the impact of emotional neglect and unmet needs on the child and they can grasp the neurobiological developmental needs of the child, they can begin to do some activities that can strengthen the areas that haven't had enough positive experience.

Strengthening the corpus callosum

There are lots of different exercises that you can do together with the child, which are fun, but also help the two hemispheres strengthen their connection. Any bilateral exercise can be helpful, such as the 'butterfly hug', which is to cross your arms over your chest and pat your shoulders whilst breathing and patting rhythmically. Another fun exercise is to stand with your feet apart and arms all the way out like a windmill, put your weight to your left foot whilst lifting your right knee and touch it with your left hand. Go back to both feet and immediately swop to the other side. Repeat this in rhythm together regularly. These exercises are called bilateral stimulation and they help the brain heal and strengthen. Marching, running, clapping games, crawling and other activities can also be beneficial.

Stories that use imagination, metaphors that can help describe and feel something and other ways of using a combination of visual image, words and an emotion can be an essential exploration to develop the area of the brain that needs further growth.

'I found other people's stories made more sense to me than when people tried to explain things without stories.'

Amber, aged 14

Self-soothing activities

When the child didn't have enough immediate and repetitive soothing when they were a baby or small child, they now need it even more so that they can 'catch up' with the development that was missed. Explore what textures and fabrics the child enjoys, and experiment with the smells they also enjoy. Put together a comfort bag for them to use when they need to intentionally feel soothed. Explore with them what touch feels positive and, ensuring it is age-appropriate and with the child having full control of the process of exploration, help them feel the feelings that their body has when they are stroked, their hair is stroked, they have hand cream, massages of the arm, they snuggle under a soft or weighted blanket. If the child is young enough, these activities can be a constant theme, even if they feel like they are 'fine now', when the next stage of development arises, they may well need to use them again, so it's best to keep them consistently available.

Vestibular practice

When the area of the brain that develops with regular swinging and larger movements didn't get enough stimulation, either in the womb or early years, it's never too late to provide the opportunity for healthy growth. Movements like being pushed in a swing, throwing and catching a ball, walking up and down slopes and steps, all provide input for a healthy vestibular system. If the child is older and they didn't have enough time and space in the presence of a nurturing adult to explore these body sensations as they were growing up, they need to do so often and regularly to help them catch up.

Relationship strengthening

The child who has experienced emotional unmet needs is now needing repetitive practice relationally, where they can explore emotions, feelings and the boundaries of relationships. They need regular, repetitive time with an adult who is therapeutic and can provide attuned, nurturing, emotionally literate, fun, soothing experiences of co-regulation on a long-term basis. They also need support to develop friendships with peers, and as many different experiences as possible, without them feeling overwhelmed, can help the child explore how they feel with their friends. It is important for the adult to offer time for reflecting on the experiences, emotions and niggles that may have been felt, in a curious, gentle, relaxed way that helps the child know you want to support them. The combination of intentional supported experience in range of relationships, with a consistent adult nurturing relationship alongside reflective curiosity would strengthen the child's understanding of friendship and relationships.

Communication of emotion

Making sense of the internal muddles that have caused the child to feel emotionally disconnected or to have the distress and turmoil of unmet emotional needs can be explored in the context of a positive, nurturing relationship.

It is important in the context of a long-term, positive, nurturing relationship for the child to explore how they feel or felt about feeling alone, abandoned, disconnected, rejected, muddled, scared, lonely, powerless, vulnerable or any other word that they may choose to explore. If those experiences are held in pre-verbal and pre-visual image years, they can be explored with positive sensory repetition of what was needed that can move into language. For example, 'When I was tiny I was left alone a lot and I think I felt sad and scared but now I know I am not alone now and have my blanket to remind me I'm safe.' If the experiences were when you were unable to care for the child and they wonder what happened, you can use age-appropriate language to gently explore how sad you were that the event happened that meant that you weren't able to soothe and comfort them like you wanted to.

These kinds of words and sentences can be used in day-to-day communication to help the child understand that you are trying to help support them:

- I'm sorry you didn't always get what you needed from me as a parent. I didn't have the tools I needed and I am really sorry. I am here now and want to try my best.

- Your opinion matters to me and I want to listen to you carefully and give you my full attention.

- I am here for you now – can you tell me what you may need from me right now? I want to support you. I know words are hard and I can wait or guess?

- My reaction or words weren't OK and I'm sorry.

- If you need to talk to me and you think I'm too busy can you find another way to let me know? I do always have time for you no matter how busy I look. You are important to me.

- I'm glad you are here and your thoughts, opinions and interests matter to me.

- I see you and hear you and I like you.

The main way that the child will recover from the impact of emotional neglect or unmet emotional needs is by the parent repetitively offering positive, nurturing, attuned relational experiences with soothing, validating attention with a positive tone of voice with soothing intonation, body language that leans in rather than away, time spent getting to know them and their interests, and verbal affirmation that you care, you are not going anywhere and you think about them all the time. Love demonstrated in specific, intentional, nurturing, felt relational warmth and care really does heal and restore over time.

Trauma recovery and the recovery from emotional neglect is possible; with a lot of relational support and nurture and repetitive experiences that can rewire the brain where it has been underdeveloped, the child can begin to dream and feel alive and connected!

APPENDIX: SOME LEGAL AND OFFICIAL DEFINITIONS OF EMOTIONAL NEGLECT

The UN Convention on the Rights of the Child

Article 19 of the UN Convention on the Rights of the Child discusses emotional neglect:

> Psychological or emotional neglect; including lack of emotional support and love, chronic inattention to the child, caregivers being 'psychologically unavailable' by overlooking young children's cues and signals, and exposure to intimate partner violence, drug or alcohol abuse. (2011)

www.unicef-irc.org/portfolios/general_comments/CRC.
C.GC.13_en.doc.html

HM Government: Working Together to Safeguard Children: A guide to inter agency working to safeguard and promote the welfare of children (2018)

The civil definition of neglect which is used in child and family law is set out in the Children Act 1989 as part of the test of 'significant harm' to a child. This is expanded upon in the *Working Together* statutory guidance which describes neglect as:

the persistent failure to meet a child's basic physical and/ or psychological needs, likely to result in the serious impairment of the child's health or development. Neglect may occur during pregnancy as a result of maternal substance abuse. Once a child is born, neglect may involve a parent or carer failing to:

a. provide adequate food, clothing and shelter (including exclusion from home or abandonment);

b. protect a child from physical and emotional harm or danger;

c. ensure adequate supervision (including the use of inadequate care-givers);

d. ensure access to appropriate medical care or treatment.

It may also include neglect of, or unresponsiveness to, a child's basic emotional needs. (HM Government 2018, p.108)

https://assets.publishing.service.gov.uk/government/ uploads/system/uploads/attachment_data/file/942454/ Working_together_to_safeguard_children_inter_agency_ guidance.pdf

Children first: The child protection system in England – Education Committee: Neglect

The Children and Young Persons Act (1933) states that:

If any person who has attained the age of sixteen years and has responsibility for any child or young person under that age, wilfully assaults, ill-treats (whether physically or otherwise), neglects, abandons, or exposes him, or causes or procures him to be assaulted, ill-treated (whether physically or otherwise), neglected, abandoned, or exposed, in a manner likely to cause him unnecessary suffering or injury to health whether the suffering or injury is of a physical or a psychological nature.

https://publications.parliament.uk/pa/cm201213/cmselect/cmeduc/137/13705.htm

United States Child Abuse Prevention and Treatment Act, as Amended, 1996

In the United States, child neglect includes physical, medical, educational and emotional neglect. Parental neglect causing physical harm through the denial of proper care or the lack of supervision is a criminal act as defined by the Federal Child Abuse Prevention and Treatment Act.

www.acf.hhs.gov/cb/law-regulation/child-abuse-prevention-and-treatment-act-amended-1996

Additional useful definitions

Emotional neglect means the failure to provide the nurture or stimulation needed for social, intellectual and emotional growth or wellbeing of an adult or child.

www.lawinsider.com/dictionary/emotional-neglect

Emotional neglect – this involves a carer being unresponsive to a child's basic emotional needs, including failing to interact or provide affection, and failing to develop a child's self-esteem and sense of identity. Some authors distinguish it from emotional abuse by the intention of the parent.

Moran, P. (2009) *Neglect: Research Evidence to Inform Practice*. Action for Children. www.basw.co.uk/system/files/ resources/basw_43707-5_0.pdf

GLOSSARY

Amygdala The amygdala is a paired structure, with one located in each hemisphere of the brain. The amygdala is in the limbic region of the brain, and it's main function is in emotional responses, including feelings of happiness and fear and anger.

Attachment This word describes the crucial relationship between two people and usually refers to the relationship between a child and their primary caregiver.

Co-regulation Refers to the process in a relationship where one adjusts themselves when interacting with another, in order to help the other become regulated.

Depersonalization The sense of being detached from, or 'not in', or feeling one's body.

Derealization A feeling that one's surroundings aren't real or the person feels like they are living in a dream-like state or things are foggy.

Developmental trauma A term used to describe the trauma experienced by people exposed to early and ongoing severe trauma. There is a set of diagnostic criteria developed by Bessel van der Kolk and his colleagues within The National Child Traumatic Stress Network in 2009.

Dissociative Identity Disorder (DID) A condition where two or more distinct states or personalities are present and 'take over' the individual. The person experiences memory loss which is more extreme than normal.

Dissociation A psychological experience in which people feel disconnected or separated from their sensory experience, emotions, sense of self or personal history.

Emotional regulation The ability to be emotionally appropriate in different settings and not be emotionally reactive or explosive.

Hippocampus There are two hippocampi, located in each hemisphere of the brain. They are seahorse-shaped and are structures mainly associated as being the memory centres of our brains.

Prefrontal cortex The part of the brain that covers the front part of the frontal lobe. This part of the brain is responsible for thinking, reflection, planning, decision making, etc.

REFERENCES

Aust, S., Stasch, J., Jentschke, S., Alkan Härtwig, E. *et al.* (2014) 'Differential effects of early life stress on hippocampus and amygdala volume as a function of emotional abilities.' *Hippocampus 24,* 9, 1094–1101.

Bowlby, J. (1973) *Attachment and Loss, Volume 2: Separation, Anger and Anxiety.* London: Pimlico.

de Thierry, B. (2015) *Teaching the Child on the Trauma Continuum.* Guildford: Grosvenor Publishing.

de Thierry, B. (2019) *The Simple Guide to Attachment Difficulties in Children.* London: Jessica Kingsley Publishers.

de Thierry, B. (2020) *The Simple Guide to Complex Trauma and Dissociation.* London: Jessica Kingsley Publishers.

Frodl, T., Reinhold, E., Koutsouleris, N., Reiser, M. & Meisenzahl, E. M. (2010) 'Interaction of childhood stress with hippocampus and prefrontal cortex volume reduction in major depression.' *Journal of Psychiatric Research 44,* 13, 799–807.

Gerhardt, S. (2004) *Why Love Matters.* Sussex: Brunner-Routledge.

Gorney, C. (2022) 'The Power of Touch.' *National Geographic,* June, 34–69.

Herman, J.L. (1994) *Trauma and Recovery. The Aftermath of Violence – from Domestic Abuse to Political Terror.* Boston, MA: Little, Brown Publishing.

Lupien, S.J., Parent, S., Evans, A.C., Trembleay, R.E. *et al.* (2011) 'Larger amygdala but no change in hippocampal volume in 10-year-old children exposed to maternal depressive symptomatology since birth.' *Proceedings of the National Academy of Sciences 108*, 34, 14324–14329.

Marshall, P.J., Fox, N.A. & the BEIP Core Group (2004) 'A comparison of the electroencephalogram between institutionalized and community children in Romania.' *Journal of Cognitive Neuroscience 16*, 8, 1327–1338.

Maté, G. (2021) *The Trauma of Relinquishment – Adoption, Addiction and Beyond.* The Ollie Foundation 2021. Video on YouTube. https://www.youtube.com/watch?v=3CW_GdFG1KY, accessed on 20/02/23.

McCrory, E., De Brito, S.A. & Viding, E. (2011) 'The impact of childhood maltreatment: A review of neurobiological and genetic factors.' *Front Psychiatry 28*, 2, 48.

Mehta, M.A., Golembo, N.I., Nosarti, C., Colvert, E. *et al.* (2009) 'Amygdala, hippocampal and corpus callosum size following severe early institutional deprivation: The English and Romanian adoptees study pilot.' *Journal of Child Psychology and Psychiatry 50*, 8, 943–951.

Mueller, S., Maheu, F., Dozier, M., Peloso, E. *et al.* (2010) 'Early-life stress is associated with impairment in cognitive control in adolescence: An fMRI study.' *Neuropsychologia 48*, 10, 3037–3044.

Music, G. (2022) *Respark. Igniting Hope and Joy After Trauma and Depression.* London: Mind Nurturing Books.

Pechtel, P., Lyons-Ruth, K., Anderson, C.M. & Teicher, M.H. (2014) 'Sensitive periods of amygdala development: The role of maltreatment in preadolescence.' *Neuroimage 15*, 97, 236–244.

Perry. B & Szalavitz. M. (2006) *The Boy Who Was Raised as a Dog.* New York: Basic Books.

Pollak, S.D., Cicchetti, D., Hornung, K. & Reed, A. (2000) 'Recognizing Emotion in Faces: Developmental Effects of Child Abuse and Neglect.' *Developmental Psychology 36*, 5, 679–688.

Schore, A.N. (2001) 'Effects of a secure attachment relationship on right brain development, affect regulation, and infant mental health.' *Infant Mental Health Journal 22*, 1–2, 7–66.

Schore, A.N. (2002) 'Dysregulation of the right brain: A fundamental mechanism of traumatic attachment and the psychopathogenesis of post-traumatic stress.' *Australian and New Zealand Journal of Psychiatry 36*, 9–30.

Shonkoff, J.P., Garner, A.S. & Committee on Psychosocial Aspects of Child and Family Health; Committee on Early Childhood, Adoption, and Dependent Care; Section on Developmental and Behavioral Pediatrics (2012) 'The lifelong effects of early childhood adversity and toxic stress.' *Pediatrics 129*, 1, e232–246.

Siegel, D.J. & Payne Bryson, T. (2020) 'The power of showing up.' POSU Refrigerator Sheet. https://drdansiegel.com/wp-content/uploads/2020/10/POSU-Refrigerator-Sheet.pdf, accessed on 20/02/23.

Szalavitz, M. & Perry, B. (2010). *Born for Love.* New York: Harper Collins.

Teicher, M.H., Dumont, N.L., Ito, Y., Vaituzis, C., Giedd, J.N. & Andersen, S.L. (2004) 'Childhood neglect is associated with reduced corpus callosum area.' *Biological Psychiatry 15*, 56, 2, 80–85.

Tottenham, N., Hare, T.A., Millner, A., Gilhooly, T., Zevin, J.D. & Casey, B.J. (2011) 'Elevated amygdala response to faces following early deprivation.' *Developmental Science 14*, 2, 190–204.

Tottenham, N., Hare, T.A., Quinn, B.T. *et al.* (2010) 'Prolonged institutional rearing is associated with atypically large amygdala volume and difficulties in emotion regulation.' *Developmental Science 13,* 1, 46–61.

Tronick, E., Adamson, L.B., Als, H. & Brazelton, T.B. (1975) 'Infant emotions in normal and pertubated interactions.' Paper presented at the biennial meeting of the Society for Research in Child Development, April, Denver, CO.

van der Kolk, B. (2014) *The Body Keeps the Score: Brain, Mind and Body in the Healing of Trauma.* New York: Penguin.

Winnicott, D.W. (1971/2005) *Playing and Reality.* London: Tavistock Publications Ltd.

Wolock, I. & Horowitz, B. (1984) 'Child maltreatment as a social problem: The neglect of neglect.' *American Journal of Orthopsychiatry 54*, 4, 530–543.

FURTHER READING

The resources listed here further evidence the impact of emotional neglect.

de Thierry, B. (2018) *The Simple Guide to Understanding Shame.* London: Jessica Kingsley Publishers.

Egeland, B., Sroufe, A. & Erickson, M. (1983) 'The developmental consequence of different patterns of maltreatment.' *Child Abuse & Neglect 7,* 4, 459–469.

Eluvathingal, T.J., Chugani, H.T., Behen, M.E., Juhasz, C. *et al.* (2006) 'Abnormal brain connectivity in children after early severe socioemotional deprivation: A diffusion tensor imaging study.' *Pediatrics 117,* 6, 2093–2100.

Kreppner, J.M., O'Connor, T.G., Rutter, M. & English and Romanian Adoptees Study Team (2001) 'Can inattention/overactivity be an institutional deprivation syndrome?' *Journal of Abnormal Child Psychology 26,* 6, 513–528.

Salokangas, R.K.R. (2021) 'Emotional neglect in childhood is common and associates with adult mental ill health.' *Nordic Journal of Psychiatry 75,* sup 1, S25.

INDEX

acceptance feelings 54–5
    see also belonging (sense of);
        confidence problems
'acting out' 38, 88–90
activities to promote
        recovery 103–8
    corpus callosum
        exercises 103–4
    relationship strengthening
        105–6
    self-soothing 43, 104–5
    vestibular exercises 105
    see also recovery from
        emotional neglect
addictions 24, 26, 67, 80–1
adolescence, anger feelings 63–4
adrenaline responses 44, 67
adulthood, legacies of
        emotional neglect 35–6
alcohol/drug addictions
        24, 26, 67, 80–1
amygdala 44, 97, 113
anger 63–4
    and outbursts 38, 88–90
anxiety 61, 67, 76
    parental 40
attachment theory 33–5, 113
attention-seeking behaviours
        35, 37, 58–9
attunement 27, 39–40, 81–2, 95

Aust, S. *et al.* 44
authoritarian parenting 24
avoidant attachment 34

babies
    importance of touch 73–4,
        76
    stress responses 78–80
being held 96–7
    see also touch
being misunderstood
        39–40, 63, 88
BEIP Core Group 20
beliefs *see* self-beliefs
belonging (sense of) 51–2
bilateral stimulation exercises
        80, 82–3, 103–4
birth trauma 25
boarding school experiences 30
bodily responses 71–84
    impact of touch 72–6
    and movement 77
    sensory sensitivity 75–6
    to food 77–8
    to stress 26, 45, 67, 78–80
body awareness 77
boundaries 57–8
    and sensory sensitivity 75–6
Bowlby, J. 33–4